ORIGINAL
VW BUS

Other titles available in the *Original* series are:

ORIGINAL
VW BUS
by Laurence Meredith

Additional research by Michael Steinke
Photography by Rowan Isaac, Dieter Rebmann and James Mann
Edited by Mark Hughes

BAY VIEW BOOKS

FRONT COVER
Immaculate 23-window Split-screen Microbus de luxe –
commonly known as the Samba – dates from 1962 and is
owned by Colin Dulson from the West Midlands, UK.
Special features of this top-of-the-range model are
aluminium trim strips dividing the two body colours of
Sealing Wax Red and Beige-Grey, further aluminium strips
along the sills, chromed hubcaps and nose motif, and
bumpers with rubber inserts.

HALF-TITLE PAGE
American-spec Bay-window version of Microbus, this time
with rare automatic transmission, dates from 1974. Jim
Mattison of Rhode Island, USA, still keeps it in daily use.

TITLE PAGE
One of the least common body variants is the Double-cab
Pick-up. This outstanding 1961 example is owned by Simon
Lewis from Yorkshire, UK, and was restored following
purchase from its original owner in Australia.

ACKNOWLEDGEMENTS PAGE
Remarkably original 1966 21-window Samba is owned by
Michael Steinke of Frankfurt, Germany. Two-tone colours
are Beige-Grey over Titian Red.

BACK COVER
The Bay-window Microbus de luxe in early form, when it
was known as the 'Clipper L'. Painted in Savanna Beige with
Cloud White roof, this 1969 example is owned by
Charles Dams of Amsterdam, Holland.

Published 1997 by Bay View Books Ltd
The Red House, 25-26 Bridgeland Street
Bideford, Devon EX39 2PZ, UK

© Copyright Bay View Books 1997

Type and design by Chris Fayers & Sarah Ward

ISBN 1 870979 84 2
Printed in Hong Kong
by Paramount Printing Group

CONTENTS

INTRODUCTION

Conceived out of necessity after World War II, Volkswagen's Transporter has evolved through four generations of vehicles into a symbol of unrivalled utilitarian excellence. During the austere but increasingly affluent days of the 1950s, there simply was nothing like it. Of course, plenty of commercial vehicles were being made all over the world – after all a wide variety of tradesmen relied upon vans and small trucks for their work – but the launch of the Volkswagen Transporter heralded the dawn of a new era, and for a number of reasons.

From the start of production of the first-generation Split-screen model in 1950 to the demise of the second-generation Bay-window Transporters in 1979 – the classic era with which we are concerned here – the VW Bus, in all its many guises, was an unparalleled success around the globe, its popularity spanning the social spectrum.

Many theories have been suggested for this vehicle's extraordinary success. It was spacious, reliable, well-made, durable and dependable – but so were the products of several other manufacturers. Volkswagen had first-class service and dealer facilities around the world for the rare occasions when spare parts were needed – but so had other manufacturers.

All the arguments in favour of the Volkswagen Transporter are indelibly printed on the minds of *aficionados* who, among the more practical, will often cite the most obvious advantages of an air-cooled engine. Others will stress that the Volkswagen was the world's first MPV (Multi-Purpose Vehicle), which was merely copied by others, including respected factories in Stuttgart and Turin. The Volkswagen is, therefore, the original and 'copies' will not suffice.

Above all these interesting arguments, however, is one factor which in my opinion sits head and shoulders above the rest. And that factor, which is arguably missing from all the others, is simply that the Volkswagen has the frontal appearance of a warm, happy, smiling, human face with which people can identify. This is not a fanciful theory based on intuition and hearsay either; it is one that is clearly supported by market research, and applies equally to the Transporter's closely related sister, the Beetle. All things being equal, it seems unlikely that any designer could ever bring prettiness to something intended as a people-carrying load-lugger with the aerodynamic properties of an average church organ, but that's precisely what Volkswagen achieved. And, to reiterate, it was out of necessity.

Today, the popularity of the Transporter is rivalled only by the enthusiasm shown for the Beetle. In Third World countries, ageing Transporters are still being used and abused for all sorts of everyday activities. No matter how scruffy and 'beaten up' they have become, old Transporters keep going for ever, even if some of the repair methods chosen to keep them on the road would not meet the legislative requirements of developed countries.

Elsewhere, Panelvans, Pick-up trucks, Microbuses and the rest are being lovingly restored, either to their original factory condition or, in many cases, to a standard capable of taking on the best in concours d'état. There are two principal reasons for this. First, restoring a Transporter, although an expensive proposition, makes financial sense when compared with the considerable cost of buying a brand new, comparable vehicle. And, second, there is in many people a simple emotion that dips strongly into unashamed, self-indulgent nostalgia – that friendly, smiling face gave the Transporter a special status with many owners. It became part of the family, and family members – no matter how worn out, nasty and recalcitrant – have endearing points that are worth preserving. Even if a new Toyota Spacecruiser, Renault Espace or similar is more powerful, more comfortable and uses less fuel.

Restoring one of these fine vehicles to original, factory-fresh condition, though, is not the relatively straight-forward job it often is with a Beetle. By definition, the Transporter was never intended as anything other than a thoroughly practical everyday machine for moving people and goods from A to B. Most led very hard lives. Thousands were scrapped, particularly Pick-up trucks which, having been especially popular with builders and similar tradesmen, were abused for years and simply died with every component completely worn out. There is nothing quite so sad in the automotive world as the sight of an ex-builder's dead Pick-up truck.

As the earliest Transporters are now getting on for half a century old, the Volkswagens of the 1950s are becoming rare. And so are some of the original spare parts that are necessary during restoration. Naturally, many bits and pieces are interchangeable with the Beetle and are, therefore, readily available, but no-one can expect to walk into a Volkswagen specialist's workshop and buy a new set of seats for a Microbus off the shelf. Six-volt batteries are also becoming harder to obtain over the counter these days.

There are scores of collectors and dealers all over the world who have all the parts necessary to rebuild even the earliest Buses, but the rarer parts are not going to be cheap, and it is often the case that not even the largest wallets will persuade some enthusiasts to part with them. Autojumbles and Volkswagen shows – and there are dozens organised throughout the warmer months of the year – are usually the best source of spare parts, and it is often possible to pick up some real bargains. Hunting for a full complement may take years, but it will prove a huge advantage to join one of the many specialist clubs, whose more knowledgeable members will almost certainly be able to help in your quest for the more elusive parts.

Luckily, air-cooled Volkswagen restorers are better served by the classic car industry than those whose enthusiasm and interests lie with other marques. Because Beetles, at the time of writing, are still being produced in Mexico, mechanical parts, especially for

Spot the differences (from top left) on 1953 Panelvan, 1966 21-window Samba, 1970 Microbus and 1978 Kombi L.

the post-1967 12-volt Bay-window models, are easy and relatively cheap to obtain. But on top of this is a huge army of specialists who make and provide good quality reproduction parts – even the normally hard-to-find pieces of body trim. All body panels and chassis parts are readily available, and most are manu-factured to a reasonably high standard, but, of course, they are not made by Volkswagen – for every repro-duction part that goes into the restoration of your

Transporter, a piece of the original vehicle will be lost for ever.

In many cases, however, this is the only option available, as many original panels just do not exist in good condition. To maintain originality, which is the whole point of recapturing the spirit of a bygone era, it is important throughout the course of any restora-tion work to preserve as many of the existing com-ponents as possible. Discarding an original Bosch dynamo because it has stopped working is unnecessary, because it can easily be rebuilt. On the other hand, some original components well and truly deserve to be binned if you actually intend to drive your vehicle.

The Michelin SDS crossply tyres that were fitted to many Split-screen Transporters should, in my admittedly very personal opinion, be cremated at the earliest opportunity and the ashes served on a plate with a large stick of celery to the person who invented the wretched things. From an entirely practical point of view, it is also worth changing the original headlamp bulbs fitted to the Split-screen Transporters for modern halogen units. Some owners have gone the whole hog and converted the entire electrical system from six to 12 volts.

Another important factor which potential restorers need to take into consideration with any Transporter model is its size. By comparison with a Beetle or any other medium saloon, the Type 2, as it was labelled at the factory, is a large vehicle. Preparing a High-top Panelvan for painting alone is a task not to be undertaken lightly, and can only be accomplished successfully by someone who is committed to the drudgery of hard work. And there are no short cuts no matter how large your budget.

And a word or two about factory originality. In many ways it is frustrating that there are no hard and fast rules where Transporters are concerned, particularly the Split-screen models, but this is in the nature of the beast. Mechanical modifications run roughly parallel to those made to the Beetle, although fewer were made to the Transporter range, but there are undoubtedly many anomalies where cosmetics and 'add-ons' demanded by customers are concerned.

Starting in 1958, major modifications were generally announced each year in August after the factory shutdown, improvements before this date having come throughout the year: significant changes, for example, were introduced on 1 March 1955. But, as with the Beetle, there is some overlap from one model year to the next, usually because the factory was obliged to use up supplies of old parts before fitting the new ones. And there is the age-old problem about the specification of vehicles differing markedly one from another to suit various markets. For example, the large bumpers with overriders fitted to Transporters sold in North America from September 1958 were also optionally available in some European countries, and a good many customers chose them as they were considered to be better looking than the standard single-blade bumpers.

As you might expect, there were also the usual mix-ups caused by good old human error. Stories about drunken stevedores sending consignments of left-hand drive vehicles to Britain are legendary, and most can be taken with a generous pinch of salt, but there is no doubt that vehicles destined for one market sometimes found their way into a quite different one, which is why their specification may not exactly tally. General wisdom dictates that 12-volt electrics were not adopted until August 1966, but this system had been available as an option since 1962, as with the Beetle. So, we can conclude from these anomalies that restoring a Transporter back to its exact factory specification may not be quite as simple as it sounds.

Another intriguing point that Volkswagen historians have not been able to agree on universally is the Transporter's name. No-one disputes the official Type 2 appellation bestowed on the range by the factory; it logically followed on from the Beetle, which was the Type 1. I have chosen Transporter as a generic term because it is a phrase that was generally used by the factory in Germany, and one that I have been used to over the past four decades. However, the Transporter has acquired different names in many countries: in Germany it is known affectionately as the Bulli, in Denmark it is the Breadvan, and many thousands of Americans simply call it the Bus. And why not? Frankly, it does not matter what you choose to call it, but I hope that the rather unimaginative 'Transporter' name used throughout this book does not offend too many readers.

The more general purpose of this book is not to argue pedantically about names, but to discover the specification of the classic Transporters that left the factory between 1950 and 1979. Some vehicles must necessarily be omitted, including Camper conversions. Apart from the fact that VW Campers form a huge subject that warrants a separate volume, no Camper ever emerged from a Volkswagen factory. The Campers from the famous Westfalia concern in Germany were officially recognised by the factory, but Volkswagen then, as now, has always been content for others to exploit that part of the leisure market. The special vehicles made for German public service organisations are similarly excluded, except in passing, because many were one-offs and it is unlikely that more than a handful are in existence today.

What Volkswagen provided was a remarkable People's *wagen*. Like the Beetle, the VW Transporter was the first and very best vehicle of its type in the world, and touched the lives of millions in the same way as the Fiat 500 in Italy, the Citroën 2CV in France and the Mini in Britain. In their way, these true People's cars helped to change the fabric of society, especially during the 1960s. With the emergence of the hippy movement during that decade, the Volkswagen Transporter was adopted almost as a symbol of freedom and peace itself, a facet recognised by Volkswagen in a recent advertising campaign to publicise the merits of the company's latest MPV developed in conjunction with Ford.

Multi-purpose vehicles, which by definition double as high-speed saloons and family hacks, are becoming increasingly popular today, their sales outstripping those of conventional motor cars in

Spot the differences (from top left) on 1953 Panelvan, 1962 23-window Samba, 1966 21-window Samba and 1978 Kombi L.

some markets. And it is not difficult to see and understand where today's designers have derived their inspiration. The crude 'box-on-wheels' philosophy that went into making the original Volkswagen Transporter is a design legacy that looks set to stay well into the 21st Century, and for many people the new breed, good as they undoubtedly are, just will not do.

Slow, noisy and thirsty – the Volkswagen Transporter may be all of these, but it has unrivalled build quality and paint finish, incomparable strength, and a soul which just cannot be found in other inanimate automotive objects. Which is why everyday Volkswagen folk around the planet are resurrecting Transporters of all types, and, in using them for the purpose for which they were intended, are recapturing a small part of the post-war era – golden to some – of road transport. As a devotee of air-cooled Volkswagens, I applaud them for their considerable efforts.

SPLIT-SCREENS (1950-67)

Once production of the Beetle was under way during the dying days of 1945, it became obvious to Major Ivan Hirst of the Royal Electrical and Mechanical Engineers, who was in charge of the factory at Wolfsburg, that some kind of internal transport was necessary for delivering components around the vast, bombed-out building. Initially, there was a small number of electric-powered vehicles but, as Beetle production stepped up, something more substantial was needed. Hirst borrowed a consignment of fork-lift trucks from the British army, but it was only a short time before he had to return them and look for an alternative.

So, Hirst got the drawing office to design a truck, a necessarily crude, simple vehicle based on a *Kübelwagen* chassis with a 'bolt-on' driver's cab. One or two were hastily cobbled together and more followed. And they did the job. Some time later, in early 1947, Ben Pon, who would become the Dutch Volkswagen importer in August 1947, paid the first of many trips to Wolfsburg and spotted one of Hirst's old machines pottering around the production lines.

It reminded him of the simple vehicles used by tradesmen in his own country, and it put him in mind of something altogether more useful. He discussed his idea with Hirst at a meeting in Minden, Westfalen,

and pencilled a simple sketch (which, incidentally, still exists today) in his notebook. The sketch was of a box-like van, and Hirst immediately agreed that Volkswagen had to make a van – Germany needed one and so, as it turned out, did the rest of the world.

Acting on Hirst's advice, Pon sought permission from Colonel Charles Radclyffe, who was in charge of light engineering in the British-controlled German zone, to put his idea into practice. Reluctantly, Radclyffe turned Pon down. At that stage the factory was struggling to survive just making Beetles, and spare manpower was too busily engaged in repairing damaged parts of the building. Resources were short and manufacturing a commercial vehicle was out of the question.

Neither Pon nor Hirst were convinced by Radclyffe's argument, and for a short time the project was put on the back burner. Then, upon Hirst's advice, Heinz Nordhoff was appointed as Volkswagen's chief executive from 1 January 1948. Hirst recognised that Nordhoff, an ex-Opel man, was a thoroughly unlikeable autocrat, but one who was capable of doing a good job. Pon resurrected his idea for a light commercial and found a more sympathetic listener in Nordhoff at a brief meeting. As a result Volkswagen's chief development engineer, Alfred

Among the earliest known Transporters surviving in good unrestored condition is this remarkable Microbus, owned by Peter Valentin – chassis number 20-09301 dates it to 31 January 1951. Retro-fitted flashing indicators are legal requirement in Germany to supplement original semaphores, while right-hand mirror has been mounted for convenience – and in Beetle fashion – on door hinge. Side views (facing page) show that Microbus, like Kombi, has only three windows on each side of passenger compartment, but seat style and interior trim panels distance this version from more austere Kombi.

Very earliest production Split-screens, those built before 20 April 1951, were without a rear window. Signwriting identifies this Panelvan, chassis number 20-02326 built on 18 August 1950, as the property of a well-known German Volkswagen collector. Until November 1950 a VW roundel was fixed where rear window was to appear. Tail-lights are post-1955 items (see page 38), but single left-hand reflector is correct for the period.

Haesner, was ordered to draw up working designs for the Volkswagen Panelvan.

By 20 November 1948 two designs, designated A and B, had been completed. They were similar apart from the cab, which on design B was slightly more rounded at the front and did not have an overhanging roof. Nordhoff preferred design B and ordered a working prototype to be constructed. By 11 March 1949 a vehicle was up and running, but it was judged something of a failure by the time testing finished on 5 April – unsurprising with the benefit of hindsight.

Because the Beetle's body was bolted to a separate chassis, it was assumed that this sound design would suffice for the Transporter. But after the test programme was halted it became inevitable that something stronger than a standard Beetle chassis, which had simply folded up under the considerable

With load space concentrated in the centre, driver and passenger up front and engine in the rear, Panelvan was well balanced and endowed with neutral handling. This example, chassis number 20-046776, dates from March 1953 and is owned by Merrill Burton. Pre-March 1955 vehicles were nicknamed 'Barndoor' owing to enormous engine lid, contrasting with small rear window. At this stage tail lamps, reflectors and centrally positioned stop light were all separate, and rear bumper was not fitted. Loading doors changed sides for right-hand drive markets, although this vehicle remained left-hand drive as it was built before Volkswagen actually engineered the steering conversion, late in 1953.

Richie King's wonderfully original Microbus de luxe (or 'Samba' or Sondermodell) was built in October 1954 and has chassis number 20-100396. It is a very early factory right-hand drive 'Barndoor', originally sold to Sweden at a time when that country drove on the left. This top-of-the-range Transporter came with four side windows, 'sky' windows, large canvas Golde sunroof, chromed hubcaps and bright trim strips dividing two body colours; by 1954 all Transporters had a rear bumper, here with rubber inserts. Until August 1963 all Sambas also had additional wrap-round windows at rear corners. Note dealer-fitted aerial position on the nose – this was the normal solution at the time.

torsional stresses imposed by the new body, would be required after all.

In what the motor industry today would regard as a laughably short period of time, a markedly different prototype was soon ready for testing. To improve torsional rigidity to a satisfactory level, the body and chassis were welded – rather than bolted – together in modern unitary construction style. No fewer than five sturdy crossmembers were welded between the front and rear axles, and there was an additional subframe incorporating two longitudinal rails to give extra beef to the structure.

There was also a change in the ratio of total weight to empty weight between the first prototype and the second – up from 1.85:1 to 1.9:1. And because the production vehicles were expected to carry heavy loads, the front axle and shock absorbers were strengthened. One thing that was not on the cards, though, was a powerful engine. Nordhoff was stuck with the 25bhp 1131cc air-cooled flat-four that

powered the Beetle. Resources just were not available to develop a more appropriate unit, but, because better acceleration was needed, yet another Porsche innovation – reduction gears in the rear wheel hubs that had seen service on the war-time *Kübelwagen* – was incorporated into the design. This modification did the trick of turning slug-like performance into acceptably brisk acceleration, but top speed remained at 50mph (80kph).

The second prototype was hammered comprehensively for some 12,000km – considered a sufficiently long test distance by Volkswagen at this stage of the company's development – before a number of other small problems were discovered. At 0.75 the drag coefficient was simply too great and did nothing to aid fuel economy. Nordhoff also suggested lowering the height of the engine bay and fitting an additional heat shield between the engine and interior luggage space by putting the spare wheel in between.

So while Nordhoff announced to the press in May

A Panelvan with windows and removable seats, Kombi was the inexpensive people-carrier. This example, chassis number 20-119731, was built on 10 March 1955 and is believed to be earliest survivor with roof peak (with new apertures above windscreen for improved cabin ventilation) that was introduced that month. Owing to US history, vehicle is fitted with clear-lens flashing indicators in place of semaphores, and sealed-beam headlights.

US Kombi began life as a School Bus, a role that required a prescribed paint scheme and detachable signs with flashing warning lamps. After active service for only a short time (mileage is just over 6000), this vehicle returned to Volkswagen factory in Wolfsburg and now lives in Frankfurt in Michael Steinke's ownership. In March 1955 the 'Barndoor' was changed for a smaller engine lid, and opening tailgate allowed access to rear luggage platform.

1949 that production of the first Volkswagen Panelvan would begin during November or December, the boys in the factory were busy constructing a further prototype that would be closer to the vehicle scheduled for production. Changing the shape of the bodywork, particularly at the front, brought the drag coefficient down to an impressive 0.44, but had the undesirable effect of increasing the top speed to 57mph (92kph) unladen or 53mph (85kph) fully loaded.

The general aim of all concerned with this project was to create nothing less than a box on wheels. With nearly two-thirds of the Panelvan's total volume taken up with 4.58cu m (162cu ft) of load space, and the ability to carry a load equal to its own weight, Volkswagen had succeeded in its aim. And Nordhoff was proud that his 'box' shaped up well. It had also been produced in a ludicrously short space of time.

The first Transporters were presented to the press on 12 November 1949. Four vehicles – two Panelvans, one Kombi and one Microbus – were on view,

and Nordhoff made an oft-quoted speech from which extracts are worth repeating here.

"Like our Beetle is a car without compromises, so will our Transporter be without compromises. This is why we did not start from an available chassis but from the cargo space. This is the clean, no-compromise principle of our Transporter. With this van and only this van, the cargo space lies exactly between the axles. In front sits the driver and in the back is the same weight due to the engine and fuel tank. That is the best compromise... We would have put the engine in the front without hesitation if this had been a better solution.

"However, the famous 'cab above the engine' gave such horrendous handling characteristics when loaded that we never even considered it. You can tell by the trees in the British zone how well the army lorries, built with this principle, handle on wet roads when they are not loaded."

The first production vehicles, all Panelvans, started

European-spec Panelvan from May 1956 (with semaphores) is chassis number 182 309, owned by Marc Maskery. A second set of side doors on the driver's side was an extra-cost option and inner door frames were strengthened from March 1955. Another 1956 Panelvan shows how bodywork lent itself well to signwriting – a great benefit to commercial operators.

rolling off the Wolfsburg assembly lines early in 1950. It was a slow start with seven vehicles built in January and three in February, but then mass-production gradually got under way with 309 vehicles built in March and April. And not once did Volkswagen look back. The Transporter was an unqualified success straight 'out of the box'. As well it might have been. By this stage, the Beetle was gaining ground in valuable export markets as a proven commodity that was already acquiring a good reputation for fuel economy, reliability and ruggedness. The dealer network offered exceptional spares back-up and first-class servicing, so the Transporter, which was sold alongside the Beetle

This US Pick-up dates from early 1958. Note low-set position of engine cooling louvres. Flatbed has 15 hardwood strips to protect metalwork, and folding sideflaps and tailgate comprise single skins attached to a framework for enhanced strength.

through Volkswagen's dealer network, had little to do to prove itself – the Beetle had paved the way. And although there was little in the way of the dealer discounts we know today – loyal customers may have been treated to a free set of mud flaps – trades people queued outside showrooms to get their hands on this innovative new vehicle.

Throughout the 17-year period in which the classic Split-screen Transporter was made, Volkswagen offered a number of models to suit different purposes. As the first model, the Panelvan, proved to be the most popular, it remained the staple diet of the range throughout. The first production Panelvans were available in European showrooms from March 1950.

In June the Panelvan (Type 21) was followed by the Kombi (Type 23, basically a Panelvan with three side windows and removable seats in the load area) and the Microbus (Type 22, similar to the Kombi but with fixed seats and better trim in the load area). In June 1951 came the Microbus de luxe or 'Samba' (Type 24), with four side windows instead of three along the passenger compartment, four 'skylight' windows on each side of the roof, a wrap-round window at each rear corner, and an even better level of trim. Trans-porters were so popular that Volkswagen was soon able to plough profits into the launch of the Pick-up truck (Type 26) by August 1952, a model that required fairly major modifications to the bodywork. Surprisingly, it was another six years before the Double-cab (or Crew-cab) six-seater Pick-up truck –

one of the most sought-after models today – was introduced, in November 1958. And for the 1962 model year there was a final incarnation of the Panelvan theme with the launch of the High-roof (or High-top) model.

As is the case with all vehicles intended mainly for commercial use, the manufacturer provided a base

Growing old gracefully and bearing the scars of hard work. Most Pick-ups, like this very original – scruffy in this case! – 1967 example led exceptionally hard lives in the hands of tradesmen, who were quick to realise that the Volkswagen could endure more punishment than any other vehicle. Note revised configuration of engine cooling louvres (introduced in August 1965), locker bed lid (with two louvres) and fuel filler flap on right-hand side, wider rear window (also introduced in August 1965) and tail-mounted Volkswagen script.

model that could be modified to suit the needs of individual tradesmen, and the list of extra-cost options – most small, some major 'custom jobs' – appears at first glance to be endless. Volkswagen itself built an ambulance (Type 27, with the rear door hinged at the bottom) and a fully kitted-out fire tender (Type 21-F). Among the many offerings from specialist conversion companies were a refrigerator van with a dry-ice blower and a mobile shop with a flip-up side panel which acted as a serving hatch, while towards the end of the 1950s there was even a tipper truck – but more of these models anon (see pages 116-119).

Like most of the world's good ideas, the Split-

screen Transporter's great secret lay in its simplicity. It was, after all, designed and built by people who judged the size of other people's wallets by their own. It had to be simple and cheap. In its austerity it perfectly reflected the age in which it was built. This was a vehicle completely without frills. And those who wanted or needed a box on wheels queued up for one at the rate of 60 per day by the end of 1950.

It is curious that criticism of the Transporter in the motoring press was conspicuous by its almost total absence – until the 1960s at any rate. But this is possibly because Volkswagen never made extravagant claims about it. The company's advertising, although typically humorous on occasions, was always straight to the point, for here was a three-quarter ton box that could carry the equivalent of its own weight without grinding to a halt, could climb a 1-in-4 hill in bottom

gear fully laden, and travel all day every day at 50mph (80kph) without complaining. It was also capable of returning an honest 20-30mpg.

All this is precisely what was required and Volkswagen duly delivered. One motoring journalist after another praised the vehicle for what it was. Almost all road tests of the 1950s verged on embarrassing – for manufacturers of small family saloon cars anyhow. Whereas journalists expected to find a crude, cheap, noisy, ill-handling 'boneshaker', what they got was a surprisingly comfortable ride, excellent roadholding and an engine that never missed a beat in extreme weather conditions – something that often could not be matched by their everyday road cars.

Because the basic package was right, the Split-screens – or 'Splitties' as they are affectionately known today – changed comparatively little down the years.

Double-cab (or Crew-cab) Pick-up production began in November 1958, six years after regular Pick-up. This example, chassis number 735 673 owned by Simon Lewis, dates from February 1961. While providing seating for up to six (with entry to rear cab through a single passenger-side door), Double-cab retained a usefully large load platform. Sequential views (facing page) show optional canvas tarpaulin, twin steel supporting bows linked by wooden longitudinal spars, and shortened load bed with hardwood strips.

Tarpaulin is secured by straps that fit into lugs and eyes; rubber bump stop protects sideflaps when they are lowered.

Customers came to regard the crudely appointed interiors as part and parcel of Transporter ownership, and few complained until the rest of the motoring world began to catch up. Some manufacturers eventually copied the Transporter and even offered new-fangled luxuries such as winding windows, but their efforts made little difference to Transporter sales.

The author of a report in *Mechanix* magazine in 1955 commented: 'Call it a Kombi, a van, or a bus, it's actually the greatest thing of its kind… The big deal, and why we are bringing you this test, is that for what it is (you name it) it's unquestionably the world's greatest buy. It's as versatile as a steamship conman and twice as useful. If you are a stickler for deluxe equipment you can, for a grand more, buy this rig with a convertible roof and observation windows for high-riding squirrels.' I concur.

BODYWORK & CHASSIS

After the collapse of the prototype's Beetle chassis under the weight of the van's bodyshell, production bodies were made integral with the chassis for improved strength and torsional rigidity. The unit is not in the manner of modern unitary construction, although Volkswagen achieved the same result, in effect, by welding the body to the chassis.

The entire structure, of course, is made of steel, all panels having been pressed cold. On the Panelvan the largest panel is the roof, which was made in one piece with a small but distinctive swage line at the front where it lines up with the division between the wind-screen halves. A conventional rain channel with an open drain at each of the four corners was fitted to the perimeter of the roof in November 1950,

The final addition: High-top Panelvan joined the range in the autumn of 1961 and proved popular with the clothing trade and the German Post Office. This is chassis number 215 107 705, built in February 1965 and owned by Peter Nicholson. Note taller side doors and raised louvres for load compartment ventilation, but standard Panelvan tailgate is retained. American-spec bumpers are fitted.

replacing the initial arrangement with a normal gutter only along the central side sections and a much smaller lip around the rest of the perimeter. Four roughly equidistant steel bows strengthen this large panel internally.

As an aside, one of the reasons why Volkswagen never officially produced a Camper version was that an extending roof, which specialist converters produced in order to provide extra headroom internally, necessitated the removal of one, or in some cases two, of these internal bows. This compromised the strength of the body structure – and Volkswagen employed lawyers who knew about product liability.

The front, or nose, panel is a partially double-skinned piece that sits immediately below the windscreen and contains the headlamp pods, which were manufactured as separate items and welded in place. It is this simply shaped and curved piece of steel, along with the headlamps and Y-shaped swage lines, that gives the Transporter its unique character. Naturally, it is no coincidence that the vehicle's frontal appearance is similar to the Beetle's.

At the base of this panel is a correspondingly curved valance and, at the top, the front panel is welded to the windscreen pillars and central windscreen division. The latter is the piece which gives rise to the Transporter's nickname – 'Splittie'.

Working backwards, there are sturdy wheelarches, a transverse foot panel that forms the floor of the cab,

and a stepped piece on which the seats are fitted. Along its rear edge, the seat panel is joined to another panel which slopes downwards to the floor of the load area. The wheelarch panels also contain a step to ease entry into the cab, and the foot panel includes cut-outs for the foot pedals and gear and handbrake levers.

In the centre of the cab immediately behind the front panel, a cylindrical pillar, which travels from the floor to just below the base of the windscreen, suffices as the heater distributor for the cab. Roughly in the centre of the seat panel is a small integral mounting for the heater control knob.

The vertical lower A pillar includes two steel brackets on each side to which the external door

hinges are attached by four large Phillips screws, and the doors themselves are fixed to the hinges with large rivets. Although the door hinges do nothing to improve the body's aerodynamic properties, their external position was a cheap solution to what Volkswagen regarded in the 1950s as an expensive engineering problem. These were also in keeping with Beetle practice: like so many other features that were interchangeable between the two models, this was important from the manufacturing and marketing points of view.

In the centre section there are slim B pillars (and C pillars on the opening door side), which are located at their bases by long outer and inner sills, or rocker panels. The B pillars contained cut-outs for the semaphore indicators until June 1960, except on US-spec vehicles which had modern flashing indicators from March 1955; after January 1961 the top hinges on the side doors were moved further down the pillar.

The central floor, which is corrugated for extra strength, is welded at the sides via a flange to the sills and at the front to a vertical panel that separates the cab from the load area. This vertical panel has a small rectangular cut-out for a window, and fresh air louvres above it. Welded to the rear part of the floor is another large corrugated panel that rises between the intrusive wheelarches, and is 'stepped' to clear the engine, fuel tank and spare wheel; the latter is mounted horizontally on a separate tray immediately below it.

The engine 'step' inevitably creates a convenient shelf for additional storage, and is welded to the inner part of the wheelarches and to the rear quarter panels,

the top half of each being double-skinned for increased structural integrity. The entire load area was painted in a rather uninspiring shade of matt grey.

Conventional in construction, the outer and inner rear wings are welded to the sills at one end and to the rear quarters along their hind edges. Above the outer rear wings, the lower side panels contain horizontal louvres – changed from vertical louvres on the prototype – which allow cool air into the engine. During production the number and configuration of louvres changed twice, although the Pick-up versions were an exception (see page 30). To begin with there were eight louvres facing outwards, but from March 1955 a ninth louvre was added. In March 1963 a tenth louvre appeared, and at the same time the louvres were modified to face inwards. It has been said that this was a safety measure, although it is difficult to understand why outward-facing vents should be less safe than inward-facing ones – in a dealer's brochure Volkswagen simply cited 'production reasons'. On Panelvans three additional louvres were cut into the two large upper side panels in order to ventilate the load area; very early Panelvans built before August 1950 lack these louvres, and for the first 12 months after their introduction the louvres were shorter than the normal style.

Common to all Transporters are the swage lines, which run at waist level across the sides of the body (or the loadbed flaps on Pick-ups) and doors; these not only break up the slab-sided appearance of the bodyshell, but also run on naturally from the Y-shaped swage lines on the nose panel.

US Microbus de luxe dating from late in the 1963 model year – the last in which 23-window version was available – has 'fish eye' front indicators (with clear lenses for US market), Westfalia roof rack, whitewall tyres, US-spec bumpers in non-original (but common) chromed finish, and 'elephant ear' mirrors.

Only two years separate these two Microbus de luxe models, but there are so many differences. The 23-window version (above), built in February 1962 (chassis number 925 219) and owned by Colin Dulson, has 'bullet' front indicators, pull-out cab door handles, outward-facing engine cooling louvres (with bright trims), and 15in wheels with slotted rims. The 21-window version (right) is owned by Trevor Mouncey and dates to April 1964 (chassis number 1 276 294): among its features are US-spec bumpers with rubber inserts, opening 'Safari' windscreens, Westfalia rack and US-spec extra pop-out windows (making six in all) for passenger compartment.

At the rear, the production vehicles were without a window in the upper panel until April 1951, when a small window, virtually useless for anything other than allowing light into the load area, was introduced. At first, the panel in which it appeared could not be opened, although an opening panel was offered as an extra-cost option (except on the Microbus de luxe).

The enormous engine lid, which is piano-hinged across the top and supported in the open position by a single, sliding stay on the right-hand side, gives early Transporters their nickname – 'Barndoor'.

To some it really is so large as to resemble a barn door, but it provides marvellous access to the engine compartment for easy servicing and maintenance.

This German-registered Samba, owned by Michael Steinke, bears chassis number 246 168 473 and was built on 13 June 1966. Rear window was increased in width on all models from August 1963, and wrap-round glass for rear corners no longer featured on range-topping Samba. Note Volkswagen badge at rear, push-button tailgate lock, and push-button with integral finger grip on engine lid.

Apart from small cut-outs for the centrally positioned stop light and opening handle, this lid has an integral pressing in the centre for the registration number plate. The engine lid is single skinned but, following Volkswagen's normal practice, it was fitted over a strengthening frame with two prominent vertical pieces attached close to the outer edges of the underside. These were drilled with eight holes in each piece to save weight.

Below the engine lid is a transverse member which sits between the two rear quarter panels. In the ordinary scheme of things this is a valance, but one which,

The end of an era. Production of the classic Split-screen Transporter finished in 1967 to make way for the Bay-window model. This beautiful 1967 Microbus de luxe was built to 'M130' specification, without a sunroof or skylight windows. Other features include US-spec bumpers and 'elephant ear' mirrors, 'short' front-mounted roof rack and accessory step below side doors. Unlike Volkswagen after 1964, its owner has highlighted hubcap motifs in black paint.

being removable by undoing two bolts and one screw on each side, has been the envy of Beetle owners for many years. By removing the bumper and this sturdy piece, the engine can be removed more easily by simply sliding it backwards on a trolley jack, thus avoiding the frustrating antics Beetle owners have occasionally encountered. This valance also contains an aperture for a starting handle, a quaint but some-times necessary accoutrement that disappeared after June 1959.

The standard Transporter (with the inevitable exception of Pick-ups) was fitted on the passenger's side with two doors, which allowed access to the load area and opened outwards. A further pair on the driver's side were available as an extra-cost option but, as they also opened outwards, caused inconvenience to owners who needed to load and unload in tight spaces. Customers' pleas for sliding doors were, in good old Volkswagen tradition, ignored for many years, but were offered as an extra-cost option from May 1963. Like the cab doors, the normal side doors were hinged top and bottom on the B and C pillars, and were made from single skins attached to simple inner frameworks strengthened with horizontal bars.

The curved cab doors were constructed in the same way, except that, unlike the Beetle, the window frames were detachable, by removing two Phillips screws at the rear, two bolts at the front and one nut in the middle. Originally, only the cab doors had concave pressings behind the door handles, the side doors not gaining these until August 1958. Cut-outs for the semaphore indicators were located in the upper B posts, but in the lower or upper B posts (depending on year) on Pick-ups.

Below floor level of the main body structure is the integral chassis frame, which, in the absence of a tunnel for a propshaft, is exceptionally strong and simple in construction. From front to rear the frame comprises a transverse box-section piece, which is curved and corresponds to the shape of the front nose panel, and is welded to the two main longitudinal chassis members. These two members run parallel to each other to a halfway point under the load area, and then open outwards towards the rear. The longitudinals contain upside-down U-shaped pieces to clear the front axle and final drive assemblies.

Behind the front curved box-section member and below the steering assembly is a short crossmember, and another similarly short but curved crossmember lies below the gearbox. Resembling a classic 'ladder' assembly, the centre section of the frame comprises five crossmembers, which bisect the two main longitudinals and are also welded to two longitudinal outriggers. At the rear of this assembly are two further stubby crossmembers, which are welded to the outriggers on their outer edges, and to the main longitudinals on their inner edges. Two square-section jacking points are welded to the chassis on each side of the vehicle.

The only complex sections of the chassis frame are close to the rear end; at the point where the longitudinals rise to clear the final drive assembly, there is a sturdy transverse tube which houses the torsion bars. Welded longitudinally to these at one end, and to the rear crossmember that runs under the gearbox, is the fork to which the gearbox itself is attached.

This layout is similar to that of the Beetle but, as the Transporter does not have a central backbone and platform chassis, none of these parts is interchangeable between the two models. The underside was normally left in grey primer, although many vehicles would have been undersealed by the dealer before delivery. Although to exactly the same design and layout, the chassis frame was strengthened in 1955.

The design of the bodyshell was retained until the end of the Split-screen era in July 1967 for two very good reasons. First, it was just about bang on in the beginning and customers throughout the world were quick to realise that sweeping modification just for the sake of it – something which Volkswagen would have rejected out of hand anyhow – was pointless. Second, the almost unimaginable sales success of the Beetle meant that the greater part of the company's efforts went into that model.

Naturally, dozens of modifications were made to the Split-screen Bus, but most were detail, under-the-skin improvements and, to be perfectly candid, its external appearance – elegant, enticing and pretty as it undoubtedly is in many respects – was as old-fashioned at the end of production as it was at the start. But, being old-fashioned is, of course, part of the Transporter's charm.

After the launch of the Panelvan, which was designed to carry goods, it was obvious that 'people carriers' would soon follow. The Kombi and Microbus arrived in June 1950, and differed from each other in their interior fittings. Because people do not actually enjoy being cooped up in the confines of a Panelvan, with or without something to sit on, Volkswagen cut square apertures in the side doors and upper side panels for windows, and removed the hardboard panel that partitioned the Panelvan's cab from the top of the seats to the roof; the bulkhead forming the lower part of this division was unchanged. In short, the Kombi and Microbus were Panelvan derivatives with three windows on each side. A Golde sliding-top canvas sunroof was an extra-cost option on these models.

The Kombi and to a lesser degree the Microbus were basic, no-frills people carriers, but it quickly became apparent to Volkswagen chief executive Heinz Nordhoff that, as prosperity returned and potential customers had more money to spend, an up-market vehicle would also be required. The Microbus de luxe (Type 24), or *Sondermodell* ('Special Model') as it was originally called, was launched in April 1951 and differed significantly from the Kombi and regular Microbus in that the body was modified to include additional windows. Four small rectangular skylights appeared along each side of the roof panel; whereas standard Kombis and Microbuses had three windows on each side of the central compartment, the Microbus de luxe had four, all of which were square; and there were two wrap-round corner windows at the rear. The nickname 'Samba' soon stuck to the Microbus de luxe, and the model built until August 1963 (when the rear corner windows were dropped) is affectionately known as the '23-window Samba' –

although it is a point for pedantic argument that there are actually 25 windows when the quarterlight and sliding window in each cab door are counted separately! A Golde sunroof was also standard on the Microbus de luxe.

One other major difference between the Microbus de luxe and the rest of the range right up to the watershed date of March 1955, when sweeping changes were made across the board, was that this model was fitted as standard with a full-width dashboard (an extra-cost option on the normal Microbus), which was stamped in a single pressing. Whereas the lesser models made do with a small, single instrument binnacle behind the steering column, the Microbus de luxe dashboard included a cut-out for the speedometer, a centrally positioned blanking piece where a radio could be fitted, and a cut-out on the passenger's side for a clock (although the clock was an

Until March 1955 – a watershed in Split-screen evolution – front of roof had a stylish crease line. After this date came a revised 'peak' with a smooth profile above and intakes for cabin ventilation below.

Panelvan rear-end contrast: single 'barn door' gave way to opening tailgate and separate engine lid in March 1955.

option when this dashboard was specified for the ordinary Microbus).

Thus far Nordhoff's draughtsmen had had a fairly easy time of it where the Transporter was concerned – resketching a Panelvan with windows was not a particularly difficult task. But, by the end of 1951, it was all eyes down towards the drawing board for a major re-think. A Pick-up truck was the next logical step in providing tradesmen – builders, carpenters and plasterers in the main – with a vehicle that would serve their purposes better.

Although the first Pick-up prototype was made in 1950, the production version (Type 26) did not appear until August 1952 and, by its very nature, caused a fair amount of head-scratching in the Wolfsburg design office. In prototype form the Panelvan had the 40 litre (8.8 Imperial gallons, 10.6 US gallons) fuel tank positioned above and to the left of the engine with the fuel filler on the outside of the left-hand rear-quarter panel, but for security reasons the filler was positioned inside the engine compartment on the production models. The spare wheel was positioned vertically to the right of the engine on the prototype and early production vehicles, but horizontally in a shallow compartment above the engine from October 1950.

For the Pick-up, therefore, both the fuel tank and spare wheel obviously had to be repositioned. The tank was reshaped, made flatter and placed above and to the right of the gearbox, while the fuel filler neck was re-routed through to the right-hand side of the body behind the locker bed and fitted with a hinged flap. The spare wheel was moved behind the driver's seat, the vertical panel that forms the back of the cab being specially shaped to house it. These useful modifications were adopted across the range from March 1955, but from August 1962 the Pick-up's spare wheel was moved to the locker bed.

Although the Pick-up was ostensibly – at least to the casual observer – a cut-down Panelvan, its production required major re-tooling at the factory. A new cab roof had to be made and was inevitably a lot smaller than the large panel fitted to the other models. The rear of the cab retained the Panelvan's small rectangular window, but the vertical panel that forms the rear cab wall, and which is attached to part of the bed, had integral convex pressings on each side of the window for added strength.

Made in two equal-size pieces, the bed was corrugated for strength, and fitted with 15 longitudinal strips of hardwood to protect the metalwork and to give extra stiffness to the bed itself. Both the sideflaps and tailgate are attached to the lower side panels of the bodywork and transverse rear panel respectively with hinges – three on each side and two for the tailgate.

Both the sideflaps and tailgate were strongly made but gained rectangular pressings (four for each sideflap, three for the tailgate) for enhanced rigidity from November 1953. Both sideflaps were fitted with a row of 'eyes' for attaching the optional tarpaulin, and with rubber bump stops on each side to protect the lower body panels from damage.

Towards the rear of the outer wings, the louvres that allow cool air into the engine inevitably occupy a lower position than those on the Panelvan, Kombi and Microbus, but perform their job every bit as well. Curiously, these eight louvres remained outward-facing after all other Transporters received ten inward-facing louvres in March 1963, but the whole pattern changed in August 1965 when nine inward-facing louvres (in three banks of three) were placed above each rear wheel arch.

Having created a useful 4.2sq m (45sq ft) of platform space, Volkswagen was not going to let the large space below it go to waste. Access to the locker bed, as it is commonly known, is provided by a door (top-hinged with two hinges) on the truck's right-hand side. The door itself is single skinned with a framework on the underside, and has a cut-out for the locking handle. Horizontal louvres are set into the middle of this door panel to provide ventilation to the lower bed, a useful feature considering that all the builders known to this author who owned these wonderful vehicles used the locker bed exclusively for storing their daily intake of bacon, eggs, sausages and bread, and a couple of shovels that sufficed as makeshift frying pans. Doubtless, Nordhoff and his team had intended this area for other objects and, to that end, provided a lower floor area of 1.9sq m (20sq ft).

In keeping with almost every other panel, the three vertical walls of the locker bed contain integral pressings, or corrugations, to give the metalwork additional strength. The beauty of this locker bed is, of course, that even with a heavy load installed inside, the handling characteristics of the Pick-up remain neutral because it is located in the centre of the vehicle.

At the rear, the Pick-up differs from the other models in that the engine lid is a good deal shorter, but, like the 'barn door', it comprises a single skin attached to a simple frame, and is attached to the bodywork with two hinges supported in the open position by a stay on the right-hand side. Like the 'barn door', the Pick-up's engine lid includes an integral pressing for the registration number plate and a small aperture for the opening handle.

Of all the Volkswagen Transporters, the Pick-up proved to be the most versatile. Apart from the canvas tarpaulin which was always an extra-cost option, Volkswagen offered a number of attachments which bolted directly onto the bodywork. They included a metal box to turn the vehicle into a mobile shop or exhibition truck, a metal ladder framework specifically designed for glaziers, and a swivelling extension ladder aimed at tradesmen and contractors who serviced city street lamps, pruned trees and attended to overhead cables. There was also a jinker, which took the form of a long boom supported by two small trailer wheels at the rear, and was used for transporting pipes, scaffolding, lumber and extraordinarily long ladders. Because of the inherent simplicity of the Pick-up's design, none of these attachments required major surgery to the main bodywork.

Until 1955 the bodywork of the range remained unaltered with the exception of the minor revisions necessary for the right-hand drive version which became available in 1953, mainly for the lucrative British market. For Volkswagen's engineering draughtsmen, the conversion to right-hand drive was fairly straight-forward, although the production engineers cursed the British as usual for obstinately insisting on driving on the 'wrong' side of the road.

Naturally the floor of the cab had to be modified with apertures on the right for the clutch, brake and throttle pedals, and the side doors on the Panelvan, Kombi and Microbus had to be moved to the left-hand side. Mirror-image dashboard arrangements were required, for both the full-width design of the Microbus de luxe and the simple instrument pod of the other models.

As an extra-cost option from 1953, Kombi and Microbus customers could order a walkway from the cab to the rear passenger compartment, contrived by exchanging the short vertical panel behind the cab seats for two separate panels. For the relatively few who specified this arrangement, there were two single seats in the cab instead of the more normal bench seat.

For the first six years of production, the Transporter was made at the main factory at Wolfsburg. It was so successful that the 100,000th unit rolled off the assembly lines on 9 October 1954, and, with sales of the Beetle beginning to escalate, it became apparent that space at the factory was getting ever tighter. A new factory was built at Hanover and Transporter production was transferred there in March 1956.

Before the move took place, however, the entire range underwent a small number of important modifications. Prior to March 1955 the Transporter's bodywork was aesthetically very simple. This is what customers expected and this is what they got, but a few voiced discontent about inadequate cab ventilation, despite the useful swivelling quarterlights in the cab's side windows, and Volkswagen came up with a very satisfactory solution – the front of the roof was gently modified to include a 'peak'. This was actually an air scoop on the underside close to the top of the windscreen which directed fresh air, via fine mesh gauze, into a steel collection-cum-distribution box on the underside of the cab roof.

This new arrangement meant that the small swage line in the centre of the roof panel disappeared – one

Various patterns of engine cooling louvres on Split-screens (clockwise from top left): eight louvres on early vehicles, and on Panelvans (except earliest ones built before September 1950) three extra top louvres for ventilating load area; nine louvres from March 1955, seen with bright trims unique to Microbus de luxe; ten louvres from March 1963, now recessed; Pick-ups were different, the first eight-louvre pattern remaining until this configuration of nine recessed louvres came in August 1965.

way of identifying pre- and post-1955 Split-screen Transporters – and the range took on a new identity which was considerably less austere. At the rear, common sense prevailed and the large 'barn door' was replaced by a smaller engine lid (with two hinges) and an opening tailgate (with a continuous 'piano' hinge), both supported by a stay on the right-hand side.

The cut-out for the rear window was still rather small at this stage, but the revised arrangement gave a

more modern look overall, as well as the practical advantage of being able to gain access to the interior from the rear. For ease of manufacture, the frames over which the side loading doors, tailgate and engine lid skins were fitted became much simpler in construction. And for convenience a finger recess was introduced in August 1958 behind the exterior handle of the side loading door – a small point but one which saved owners from trapping their knuckles.

After the move to Hanover, where Volkswagen employed a workforce of 5000 and stepped up Transporter production to 250 units per day, the design office had a break, principally because of the disruption of moving from one factory to another, and partially because it had run out of new ideas. Sales were increasing and Nordhoff was as keen as ever to capitalise on the company's almost unbelievable success. Because the Beetle was due for a larger rear window and several other modifications, the Transporter range remained largely unchanged except that the engine lid pressing above the registration plate was slightly modified in May 1958 when the centrally positioned brake light was dropped.

The Pick-up was optionally fitted with a wooden platform attached to the main bed from 21 October 1958. A day later the wide-bed Pick-up was announced. This was but a variation on the Pick-up theme, and because 'wide-beds' were mainly aimed at the building trade, they are incredibly rare today (as an aside, the only presentable survivor known in the world was considered for photography for this book, but did not emerge from the paint shop in time). Like the regular Pick-up, the wide-bed was similarly available with the extra-cost option of a canvas tarpaulin.

On 3 November 1958, just a couple of weeks after the wide-bed Pick-up went into production, yet another variation on the Pick-up theme began to be assembled at the Hanover plant. This was the desirable and amazingly useful Double-cab Pick-up, or Crew-cab as it is popularly known in North America. The launch of this vehicle is particularly interesting for social historians because it coincided with massive building programmes instituted by virtually all governments in the Western world.

Post-war prosperity had arrived; people demanded and could afford new homes, larger gangs of builders and allied tradesmen were needed to construct them, and Volkswagen cashed in on the boom by providing another utility vehicle with seating for up to six people. The idea, however, was not Volkswagen's: a 'crew-cab' had been built as a Pick-up conversion since 1958 by Karosseriefabrik BINZ of Lorsch, Württemberg, and had sold so well that Volkswagen saw a market for its own version.

With an extension to the standard Pick-up's cab, the Double-cab was fitted with a new roof panel, slim but strong B posts behind the front cab doors, and an additional door for rear passengers on the opposite side to the driver. This new door was externally hinged with two hinges and had a concave pressing behind the door handle. Both this door and the fixed panel on the opposite side contained a window.

Behind the rear passenger door, and on the opposite side of the cab, were new upper and lower panels divided by two prominent swage lines, and a larger panel – with a rectangular rear window – that formed the rear of the cab. Again, this rear wall contained integral pressings, or corrugations, for strength.

Three Panelvan load compartments, from 1953 (top), 1956 (centre, with doors on both sides) and 1965 (bottom, in High-roof form with some internal trim). Grey painted panels are mostly corrugated to enhance body rigidity, while High-roof's extra height – and 42cu ft more space – is clearly seen. Spare wheel configuration is different on all three: initially it was on a shelf over the engine, with higher platform above; from 1955 it moved behind cab seats, requiring a special well in the dividing wall; from 1962 introduction of separate driver's seat caused a more substantial intrusion into load compartment.

As the new cab obviously took up a good deal of rear platform space, the Double-cab had a half-size locker bed below and behind the rear compartment, with access under the bench seat – safe and secret! The Double-cab model proved to be so popular that Volkswagen went on to make an equally successful Bay-window version when the range was completely revised in August 1967.

Bodywork modifications to the Double-cab were few and far between from its launch to the end of production. Very early in 1959 the B posts lost their apertures for the familiar semaphore indicators as more modern flashing indicators were fitted to the front panel, fully 18 months ahead of other Transporter versions sold in Europe. In August 1962 the spare wheel well was made deeper, because the driver's seat was separated from the bench seat that had characterised the cab previously, and was also made adjustable for reach.

Autumn 1961 saw the launch of the final model in the range in the form of the High-top, or High-roof, Panelvan. Although the High-roof was listed as a separate model in Volkswagen's advertising literature, it was actually nothing more than a standard Panelvan with, as its name suggests, a higher roof, for which the standard upper side panels and side doors needed to be deepened.

With its extra load volume, the High-roof soon attracted an important customer in the form of the German Post Office, and it was also popular with companies in the clothing trade. And within a short time these vehicles could be seen all over Europe and North America being used as mobile take-away cafés fitted with a top-hinged serving hatch on the opposite side to the side doors.

As an aside there was one particularly exciting use that Transporters were put to during the 1960s, and I hope that readers will forgive a brief but personal recollection of these vehicles. Plush American motorhomes are commonplace in the paddock at Grand Prix races today, but 30 years ago a number of competitors used Volkswagen Transporters, especially Pick-ups, for carrying not only their tools and spare parts from meeting to meeting, but for also transporting their racing cars. The sight of a Brabham or Lotus nosecone poking out through a crudely-cut hole in the rear of a Panelvan, or from the rear of a Pick-up with a protective cover over it, was common. Today, of course, there is as much interest in restoring Transporters as there is in rebuilding the exciting racing cars they carried. Maybe one day an example of each will be reunited.

As the volume of traffic increased in the 1960s, it became apparent that the small rear window fitted to each model did not give much of a view of following vehicles so, in August 1963, Panelvans, Kombis and Microbuses were fitted with a much wider rear window (Pick-up versions, however, had to wait until August 1965 for the cab rear window to be similarly

enlarged), and the tailgate was also widened at the same time. As a result, the upper quarter body panels decreased in size and wrapped around the rear to a lesser degree than previously. At the same time the rear quarter wrap-around windows of the Microbus de luxe were dropped altogether because of the lack of space for them – hence this later top-of-the-range model has become known as the '21-window Samba'. Along with the new tailgate, there was a finger indent in the narrow panel below the tailgate to allow it to be lifted now that a simple push-button lock replaced the previous T handle; this finger indent was deleted in August 1966 when the tailgate push-button received a finger grip for the last year of production.

From the front the Transporter looked the same as ever – unassuming, pretty and distinctive – but from the rear the new tailgate and wider window gave it an altogether more modern look and feel. It became entirely in keeping with the 1960s – bright and light. Curiously, the division between the two windscreen halves remained intact until the end of Splittie production. Although no-one really knows why this pre-war relic was kept while other features were modernised, the answer is almost certainly down to Nordhoff having found a style for the Transporter that worked, and using this as an excuse for not investing in a one-piece windscreen.

Porsche used a split windscreen on its early 356 sports cars because funds were not available for a one-piece item. Volkswagen used a one-piece windscreen on the Beetle throughout its production life, but the Transporter used two pieces of Sekurit's best toughened glass right up until 1967. Some Volkswagen enthusiasts believe that the shape of the Transporter's glass area – in its entirety – was modelled on a German war-time Messerschmitt bomber, and legend has it that this style was preferred for the Transporter as a defiant gesture of a defeated regime. But, along with all the other myths that surround post-war Volkswagen history, this one can probably be dismissed as the product of imagination.

Overall, the design of the body was exceptionally well thought out, a fine example of a no-nonsense approach in providing the commercial market with what it really needed. But if the draughtsmen and production engineers had performed their side of the bargain well, the people working on the factory floor deserve equal credit for the way in which they executed the technical drawings. The build quality, panel fit and paint finish were only matched by the Beetle in the world of automotive mass production. The Transporters of the 1950s were fairly basic, even in top-of-the-range Microbus de luxe form, but the workmanship that went into making them was of such an extraordinarily high standard that many survive today despite having covered 'starship' mileages. And this is just one reason why restoring bodywork to an equal standard is both challenging and costly.

BODY TRIM

When production of the Beetle finally got under way in August 1945, it was necessarily austere and even crude in its fixtures and fittings. This was largely the result of difficulties in securing regular supplies of raw materials, but by 1950, when the Transporter was launched, supplies of components and raw materials had improved beyond recognition. Yet the Panelvan was almost equally austere.

It need not have been, but it is an endearing and enduring characteristic of all Germanic races that they can, when needs must, be brutally practical, possessing an almost obstinate, in-built mechanism that inherently leads to a stoic refusal to enjoy the aesthetic appeal of admittedly unnecessary items of body adornment. The prototype Panelvan was dreary in the extreme, the black-painted headlamp rims, bumpers and hubcaps giving the appearance of a crudely painted child's toy.

Nordhoff realised that even the least cultured bricklayer's mate would raise an eyebrow or two if confronted with such an uninspiring confection. So, between prototype and production a few concessions, although not too many, were made to the dewy world of aestheticism. As one early Volkswagen advertisement made clear: 'Mit ihm fährt der Erfolg' (Success rides with him). And to create the right image for 'him', the Transporter was fitted with what some people at Volkswagen considered to be fancy frills.

At the front, the most prominent item of trim was the large V-over-W emblem in the middle of the nose panel. Made of aluminium until April 1951 and steel thereafter, these motifs were usually finished in white, although the top-of-the-range Microbus de luxe always had a chromed version. The body colour finish often seen on these emblems today may on occasion have originated from the factory or the dealer, but are normally the result of owners wishing to cheer up the appearance of their vehicles.

The Bosch or Hella headlamps look like Beetle units turned through 90 degrees, but they are not: they differ in having their two beam adjuster screws in different positions, the addition of a small drain hole at the bottom, and very different lenses. They are each attached via a black plastic insert with a single Phillips screw located halfway up the inboard side of the rim, close to one of the beam adjusters. The rims themselves were chromed on all models, although grey paint was used on occasion in the first three years of production during periods when supplies of chromed rims faltered.

Like the Beetle, the front bumper on the Transporter was a different shape from the one at the rear – and a rear bumper did not appear, except as an extra-cost option, until 10 March 1953. This date, coincidentally, is when the Beetle's 'split' rear window was changed for the famous 'oval' unit. Even then a rear bumper was standard only on the Microbus de luxe and Pick-up, and was not fitted across the range until April 1954. Similar to early 356 Porsche items, the single-blade front bumpers were rather elegant to start with, and curved around the lower valance and below the cab doors. They had a convex pressing at their centres – often highlighted in a different colour from the rest of the blade – with a blank in the centre where the registration number plate was attached. The rear bumper, which was also a single blade, curved more sharply around the base of the rear quarter panels and stretched as far as the wheelarches. For both bumpers, rubber inserts with bright surrounds were fitted as standard to the Microbus de luxe, and available as an option on other models.

Both bumpers were supported by steel hangers, which travel through the valances and are bolted to the chassis legs. For the North American market from

Large VW roundel on front panel was subtly changed in April 1951. Before this date it was made of aluminium (left) and had fairly 'softened' contours. Steel version used after this date (centre and right) had a crisper shape and a linking piece between the V and W. Microbus de luxe always had chromed roundel to complement its bright trim strips.

Bumper evolution, in each case with and without Microbus de luxe rubber inserts: early bumper had separate centre pressing, often painted white to contrast with body colour background; stronger 'one-piece' bumper from August 1958 always came in silver white paint; American-spec bumpers had overriders and nudge bars (but the overrider rubber seen bottom right is an after-market addition).

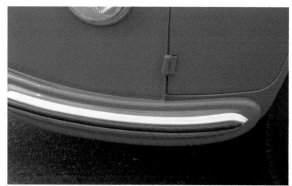

Unlike earliest Beetles, Transporters had two SWF windscreen wipers from beginning of production, but they were just as skimpy. Paint finish was black on 'utility' versions (left), satin metallic grey on people-carriers (centre). Bodywork changes in March 1955 included a slightly different nose panel, with indents for the wiper spindles (right).

Circular rear-view mirror was fitted in a special mounting on windscreen pillar on early vehicles, pointing upwards initially (left) but downwards from July 1952 (above); after March 1955 it dropped to door hinge and pointed upwards again (right).

September 1958, there were what are universally known as the 'American-spec' bumpers. These comprise a lower blade with tall overriders and an upper bar passing through the top of the overriders. Their purpose was to offer extra bodywork protection in tight parking spaces, and many thought them to be so attractive that it was not long before they were commonly fitted to Transporters all over the world. These bumpers also came with the option of protective rubber inserts with bright surrounds, a feature that was standard on the Microbus de luxe.

Stronger bumpers without overriders, similar to the basic appearance of the US bumpers but with longer blades, were introduced on European-spec vehicles in August 1958, and again the availability of bright-surround rubber inserts remained. Throughout Splittie production, the bumpers fitted to all models, including the Microbus de luxe, were painted silver-white (code L82), although nowadays many vehicles sport chromed items.

The design of the front quarterlights changed in January 1953. The first type was 'piano-hinged' along its entire front edge, and operated by a 'scissor' catch with a screw knob in black plastic. The familiar type swivels at a roughly central point top and bottom, and is held shut by a handle normally painted black but chromed on the Microbus de luxe.

All European-spec Transporters were fitted until June 1960 with semaphore indicators, which had amber lenses and were operated by solenoids mounted at the top of each unit. Even on the rela-

Made by SWF, semaphore indicators were solenoid-operated and protruded from the B posts; there were two different patterns, the change from 'ribbed' to 'smooth' having occurred in early 1953.

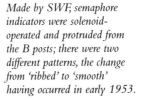

Flashing indicators of 'bullet' type at the front replaced old-fashioned semaphores from March 1955 for the US) with clear lens) and June1960 for Europe (with amber lens).

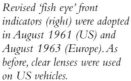

Revised 'fish eye' front indicators (right) were adopted in August 1961 (US) and August 1963 (Europe). As before, clear lenses were used on US vehicles.

Legal requirements meant that European headlamp pattern (left) was replaced by a sealed-beam version (below) for US market.

tively congestion-free roads of Europe in the 1950s, however, it was becoming obvious that modern flashers would have to be fitted, as they were more easily seen by other road users.

The new flashing indicators, which were fitted to American-spec vehicles from March 1955, were placed on the front panel above the headlamps and, because of their distinctive shape, became known as the 'bullet' type. European vehicles had amber lenses while those exported to America had clear ones. However, this style of flasher did not last long. Consumer groups, particularly in safety-conscious America, argued that the bullet-shaped lenses posed a potential hazard to pedestrians, so they were replaced at two dates, August 1961 (US) and August 1963 (Europe), by large-diameter round indicators with pedestrian-friendly lenses, known as the 'fish eye' type. Again, the American-spec indicators were clear and the European models had amber lenses. Both the 'bullet' and 'fish eye' types were seated to the bodywork with black plastic inserts, but only the later type had a chromed perimeter to the lens.

Supplied by SWF, the windscreen wipers – and some journalists expressed surprise that there were two – carried comparatively short rubber blades (but longer than those of the Beetle) resembling a Christmas tree in section. The wiper arms were painted black, although Kombis and Microbuses had a satin metallic grey finish. Longer and stronger wiper arms and blades appeared across the range from August 1963. Being fitted on the front panel below

Tail-light evolution: until March 1955 (top left) tail-light had wide chromed bezel, with this 'bubble' lens in 1954-55 but flat lens (incredibly rare nowadays) before that, always with separate reflector below; March 1955 to May 1958 style (top centre) has thinner bezel and integral reflector with hexagonal outline, and incorporates indicator function for US market; rectangular central stop light (centre) was used until May 1958, with number plate light below; larger lens (now including stop light) and lugged bezel for May 1958 to August 1961 (top right), normally with integral flashing indicator when appropriate but here – on Australian-sourced vehicle – unusually supplemented by separate indicator; large unit from August 1961 (far left), with US-market red indicator segment; European alternative (near left) has amber indicator segment, plus other lens differences.

the windscreen from the beginning of production, the wipers were considered to be rather modern for the time, as so many commercial vehicles had their wipers located at the top of the windscreen.

The wipers sweep the glass parallel to each other and are sited with a left-hand drive bias to park on the left. They were never repositioned to offer an advantage to the owners of right-hand drive vehicles, which is why a segment at the bottom right-hand side of the windscreen remained unswept, despite persistent criticism from owners and journalists alike. Volkswagen argued that tooling up for the conversion would have been too expensive, but this is implausible in view of the profits the company was making. Again, it seems probable that this was a little protest against the few countries that chose to drive on the left-hand side of the road, an eccentricity that continues to bewilder Europeans to this day.

A circular mirror was fitted as standard on the driver's side on commercial vehicles, a second one appearing on the passenger's side from October 1956. Located on angled arms with a bracket on the windscreen pillar, they initially pointed upwards; in July 1952 the arms were changed to point downwards; and in 1955 they were screwed into the cab door hinges and pointed upwards again. Quite extraordinary!

The cab door handles were shared with the Beetle.

Pull-out cab door handle (right) with integral lock on driver's side was replaced in December 1963 by a fixed version (below right) with circular push-button and integral lock on both sides; with later style, adjacent side door contains a recess to avoid handle damaging the panel.

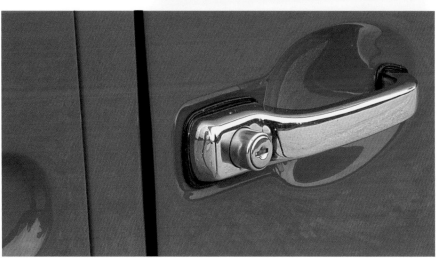

Curved in section and tapering almost to a point on their front edges, these handles were chromed to an exceptionally high standard across the range, and had an integral lock on the driver's side only. Separate keys were supplied for the door locks and ignition – a minor irritation which characterised almost all German motor cars until well into the 1960s.

To release the door's locking mechanism, the earlier type of handle needed to be pulled away from the door, but this rather old-fashioned arrangement was replaced in December 1963 by a fixed handle with a round push-button. Both types of handle were seated to the door skin by a black plastic insert. The side doors to the load – or passenger – compartment were fitted with rather larger, most workmanlike handles, which were lockable from the inside from 1962 and so sturdily made that even seasoned owners needed to summon Cossack-like strength to operate them. There were three designs of handle over the years: until March 1955 a tapered shape of handle had a separate lock escutcheon below it with a sliding dust cover; the second type of handle, used until December 1963, had a similar shape but the lock became integral, and a finger recess was incorporated into the door panel from August 1958; the final design had a rather more 'square' appearance, matching the new cab door handles that were adopted at the same time.

At the rear, the 'barn door' was opened with a chromium-plated T handle, which had an integral lock and seated on a black rubber insert. A T handle also opened the new tailgate from March 1955 to August 1963, but this handle was of lighter construction and subtly different design, with extended tips and a 'finger groove' along its rear side. The T handle changed to a circular push-button lock in August 1963, and an indent in the bottom of the tailgate gave the necessary finger room to lift it. This modification was clearly in keeping with modern times, but an indication that elements of the Split-screen's character were beginning to be lost. Yet another change occurred in August 1966, only a year before the end of production, when a push-button with integral finger grip was introduced, so that the indent in the panel below was no longer required.

After March 1955 the smaller engine lid was no longer opened by a T handle, but by a special 'church key' which was inserted into a square hole within a circular chromed fitting with a sliding, spring-loaded dust cover. The same fitting was also used for the Pick-up's locker bed. Pleasing design though this was, it must have been expensive to manufacture, so from August 1965 the engine lid was opened by a circular push-button combined with a finger grip below. From the same date the Pick-up's locker bed continued to use the previous 'dust-cover' fitting but now with a conventional lock inside; to have fitted a projecting handle here would have almost certainly led Ralph Nader and company in the direction of a maternity clinic to give multiple birth.

The rear lights were made specially for the Trans- porter, so their expense must have made old man Nordhoff bite hard on his breakfast bran flakes for a while. At first they had smooth, flat lenses with wide, chromed, circular bezels, but a convex 'bubble' lens was fitted from 1954. At this stage the brake light was a separate rectangular unit mounted above the number plate and fitted with a red lens. Just below the brake light, on the underside of the barn door's inte- gral number plate pressing, was a rectangular lamp with a clear Perspex lens for illuminating the number plate; the Pick-up truck had a similar arrangement. Initially, a circular red reflector with a narrow chromed bezel was positioned below the left-hand tail lamp; after March 1952 another was fitted on the opposite side. Except for the number plate lamp, all rear lights were fitted with a black plastic insert.

Slightly different tail lamps with thinner chromed bezels and flat lenses with a 'hexagon' reflector pattern came at the major change point in March 1955, and for US vehicles without the old-fashioned semaphore indicators these lamps also incorporated the indicator function. The central brake light was finally dropped in May 1958, so brake lights now appeared in larger tail lamps, whose chromed bezels included two lugs for exposed screws; as before, these units also included indicators where appropriate. In August 1961 the tail lamps were enlarged again to include an amber (Europe) or red (US) segment at the top for the flashing indicators that were now fitted for all markets. Red reflectors featured in the centre of these units, and the stop and tail lamp function was at the bottom. This last type was roughly rectangular in shape but with the four corners nicely rounded off, and they were fitted to the bodywork with black plastic inserts.

Body adornment, as might be expected, was spartan on the lesser models and they looked none the worse for it, but the top-of-the-range Microbus de luxe was an altogether different kettle of fish. The differences between the Microbus de luxe and the other models were much the same as those between the Standard and de luxe (or Export) versions of the Beetle. Volkswagen's philosophy was simply that it would provide a basic Kombi, perfectly capable of carrying goods or people, but, if you wanted fashion- able accoutrements, they would be offered but – in true German fashion – at a price.

To this end the Microbus de luxe had anodised aluminium-alloy mouldings running along both swage lines on the front panel, and across the sides below the windows and wrapping around the rear quarter panels. Plastic beading, self-coloured to match the lower body colour, was fitted along the centre of these mouldings. Further aluminium-alloy moulding strips were attached to the outer sills (or rocker panels), bumpers and outward-facing engine cooling louvres (until March 1963).

These brightwork mouldings had a dramatic effect

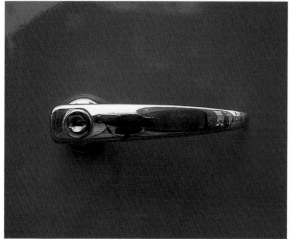

There were three styles of turning handle for the aft side door: until March 1955 handle (above) has lock escutcheon below, with sliding cover; second type (left), to December 1963, has integral lock, and finger recess in panel from August 1958; final design (below left) has squarer appearance, and finger recess in panel is seen.

Five different locking styles featured at the rear over the years (from top left): 'solid' T handle used on 'Barndoor' engine lid, until March 1955; then revised (and lighter) T handle, with turned-back tips and 'finger furrow' behind, opened separate tailgate until August 1963; tailgate push-button, with finger indent in panel below, followed until August 1966; from March 1955 to August 1965 smaller engine lid was opened by a 'church key' inserted into a hole with sliding dust cover; for last two years of production engine lid was opened with this push-button with combined finger grip, a design also adopted for the last year of production for the tailgate, with the finger recess in the panel below deleted as a consequence.

on the Transporter's appearance, and made some sort of social statement about its owner. The Microbus de luxe was most definitely not a tradesman's vehicle, in the same way that the Karmann-built Beetle Cabriolet stood aside from the 'common' Beetle herd, although in Germany these smart station wagons saw a great deal of service as taxis, especially at airports.

One of the most desirable features is the full-length Golde sunroof, which was an extra-cost option on the Kombi and Microbus but standard on the Microbus de luxe. Made of a closely-woven canvas material, this was of the slide-back variety that simply folded backwards into loops. The sides of the sunroof ran in aluminium channels and the assembly was secured in the closed position by a central latch at the front.

Those owners who wanted a Microbus de luxe for less money could order one with 'M130' specification, lacking the sunroof and skylight windows. These vehicles very often went to US customers.

INTERIOR

Anyone who drove or travelled as a passenger in a Split-screen Transporter when they were new was more likely to be inspired by what they saw through the large windows rather than what they encountered in the cab or rear passenger compartment. But the spartan nature of the Volkswagen, utilitarian as it was always intended to be, certainly compared favourably with commercials made by other manufacturers.

In the 1990s, when even the most basic multi-purpose vehicle would not stand a chance in the marketplace if it lacked a plethora of electric gadgets and plush velour upholstery, it is easy to forget that 40 years ago the world was a very different place. During the 1950s the average commercial vehicle, light van or heavy truck – and none could honestly be compared with the Volkswagen – was a noisy, slow and uncomfortable means of transporting cargo. Their cabs were severely lacking in creature comforts. The seats were

ghastly and guaranteed to promote backache. And with a large, impotent diesel engine throbbing by the side of the driver's knee, the vibration alone was enough to convince most people that the Volkswagen Transporter was comparatively civilised.

In the cab, the non-adjustable three-man bench seat was a simply constructed steel frame affair with light padding and a fine-grained black vinyl covering. Although soft cloth was used for Beetles of the early 1950s, Transporters were always trimmed in vinyl as this material was infinitely more practical and easier to clean – an important consideration for commercial operators. For the 1963 model year, the driver's seat became separate, had a more comfortable curved backrest, and was adjustable fore and aft with a handle on the outside of the cushion. The seat was guided in conventional rails welded to the seat panel below. At the same time the backrest and squab of the passenger seat were made to fold forwards and down but the seat was not adjustable.

Commanding driving position, but the interior – this is a 1953 Panelvan – is typically austere, the firm bench seat upholstered in plain black vinyl. Passenger 'safety measures' comprise a foot bar and grab handle.

Contained within a simple binnacle, the early VDO speedometer – calibrated to only 80kph or 50mph – has a needle that charmingly appears to run 'backwards'. This elegant, large-diameter, three-spoke steering wheel was used until 1955; it was normally black, but ivory on the Microbus de luxe, with the speedometer backing panel and switches (for wipers and headlamps) in matching colour.

For the cab door panels of the Panelvan, Pick-up and Kombi, plain fibre-board was screwed to the inner door frame, and a small oddments bin was cut into each until the autumn of 1960. The floor panel was covered with a hard-wearing one-piece rubber mat with fine longitudinal ribbing. The mat was normally self-coloured in black, although on late Microbus de luxe models similar dark colours were used to suit the lower body colour that was chosen.

All 'Barndoor' models had a painted tubular steel foot bar attached to the cab floor on the passenger's side. Seat belts were rarities in the early 1950s – it is difficult to think of any car or commercial that had them fitted during this period – and conventional

Volkswagen wisdom dictated initially that a solid dashboard-mounted grab handle was appropriate on 'Barndoor' models for preventing front passengers from unwelcome high-speed travel through the windscreen in an impact. From March 1955, however, even this concession to safety was dropped from the new full-width dashboard, but in July 1961 a revised grab handle – now a flexible one – appeared once more.

The Kombi's seats in the rear passenger compartment were constructed in the same way as those in the cab with a simple steel framework, but they had deeper cushions, were more generously padded and had the same type of plain, finely grained vinyl covers. These seats, however, differed from those in the cab in that they had tubular steel legs to raise their height, and were attached to the floor with easily detachable butterfly nuts. Unlike the early Panelvans, the Kombi did have a rubber mat on the floor of the rear passenger compartment.

It is stressed that this is how Kombis left the factory. Those that were converted to Campers by private specialists were, in many cases, very plush and included high quality carpeting and full headlinings throughout. Indeed the interiors of some conversions were every bit as pleasant and comfortable as the sitting room of a well-kept house. But Volkswagen did not get involved with Campers, so they are outside the scope of this book.

By contrast with the less expensive models, the Microbus's interior was slightly more luxurious. Both versions of the Microbus, Type 22 and Type 24, were fitted with a full headlining from front to rear that also extended to the area around the side windows. Initially, it was made of a soft cloth material, but white vinyl with tiny perforations was an extra-cost option from May 1964 and standard from September 1964. These were the same materials that were fitted to the Beetle, the change on both models taking place at the same time. Apart from being much easier to clean, the white vinyl had the effect of brightening up the interior and giving it an altogether more modern feel that was in keeping with contemporary trends.

Panelvans, Pick-ups and Kombis had a plain hardboard headlining in the cab. Panelvans and Kombis had no headlining of any sort in the rear, the body colour roof panel sufficing for these more basically appointed models. The spartan character of the Kombi was completed by bare metalwork around the side windows and below the waistline, unlike on either of the Microbus models.

Whereas the Panelvan and Kombi lacked interior side and door panels in the load-cum-passenger area, Type 22 and Type 24 Microbuses had vinyl covers, mostly in two-tone colours with anodised alloy mouldings – three in all – separating the colours. Microbuses were also treated to a large ashtray on the wall between the cab and the passenger compartment, and de luxe versions had a chrome rail around the outside of the rear luggage compartment for securing luggage. The wall separating the cab from the passenger area in the Microbus was covered in vinyl.

For passenger-carrying Transporters, the seats in the rear were laid out in two rows. Both were three-seater benches, the central row having a tipping back-rest for the seat nearest the door, in order to aid entry to the rear bench. As an option (for less cost) a narrower two-seater central bench could be ordered. The central seats on both the Kombi and the Micro-buses were fitted with grab handles – tubular steel until October 1963, ridged plastic thereafter – on the tops of the backrests for the benefit of passengers in the rear. The earlier type of grab handles were painted ivory on the Microbus de luxe but black on other versions, in each case with polished alloy ends secur-ing them to the seat backrests. Both of the Microbuses were also fitted with armrests attached to the interior body panels for occupants of the outer seats.

Plain vinyl was used for the passenger seat covers in Kombis, but the Microbus seats were pleated and piped. Both types were on the hard side of firm in typically German fashion, which is why they are generally so durable. In recent times, several Microbus owners have upgraded their seats by fitting leather covers and, as smart and comfortable as they undoubt-edly are, leather was never officially fitted at the factory. However, it seems likely that a number of unofficial vehicles did leave the factory with leather upholstery to special order for favoured customers. Volkswagen also kept special vehicles for use by distinguished guests, and it is possible that these were more plushly appointed than standard vehicles. But there is nothing in official records to suggest that anything other than vinyl was used.

The interior heating system has always been a bone of contention because some argue that it is simply not adequate. Cab heating is provided across the range by the vertical tube, or cylinder, behind the front panel and is operated by a handle. The flow of heat is controlled by a black or ivory-coloured plastic turning knob located on the panel between the cab floor and the seat. The luxury of heating in the rear passenger area was standard on both types of Microbus but optional on the Kombi – and even Panelvans could be ordered with heating for the load area! Situated below the rear bench seat, the heater outlet comprises a long, horizontal, cylindrical tube with a series of slots to allow hot air from the exhaust heater box system to escape into the cabin.

For all models, Volkswagen offered an alternative system of rear compartment heating in the shape of the Eberspächer petrol heater, which, of course, was also an extra-cost option – and an expensive one. These quaint devices, which run on petrol from the vehicle's main fuel system, were intended for use when the vehicle was stationary for long periods with the engine switched off. They were exceptionally effi-cient in principle, but in practice they proved to be uncharacteristically unreliable and were necessarily

The high seat position dictates that the pedals, headlamp dipswitch, steering column, gear lever, handbrake and heater tube rise almost vertically from the floor. On the panel directly behind the gear lever are the black plastic rotary heater control and smaller manual choke control knob. Both views are of a 1953 Panelvan.

complex – a typical example of the way in which Volkswagen occasionally attempted to scratch its left ear with its right hand.

Critics often comment that the heating system is totally useless – which is entirely untrue. It is extremely efficient and possesses the ability to 'cook' passengers, even in sub-zero temperatures. At its

conducting heat from the engine to the cabin, are expensive, so owners tend to buy cheaper, non-genuine alternatives which do not have the same internal thermo-dynamic properties. As always you get what you pay for.

A sun visor, initially made of grey fibreboard, was fitted to the driver's side as standard on all models. From July 1958 Microbuses were fitted with a padded, vinyl-covered visor in the interests of safety, and from August 1961 all models received two of them.

Until August 1965, the interior cab door handles, similar to those fitted to the Beetle, were shaped like a banana. For the first 10 years they were chrome-plated on all models, but from the autumn of 1960 the finish became white paint on all but the Microbus de luxe. From August 1965 there were shorter, chunkier handles in white plastic (or chromed metal on the Microbus de luxe). The side windows in the cab were always of the sliding (rather than winding) variety, and are operated by a simple chromed finger latch. Until January 1953 the opening quarterlights were piano-hinged to the window frames along their leading edges, but swivelled on a pin top and bottom there-after. The quarterlight catch also changed to suit, from a scissor type with a screw-tight black (or ivory on Microbus models) knob to a more conventional finger latch with a push-button.

In March 1955 the cab roof was restyled to allow for the installation of an interior fresh air system. This took the form of a simple metal box mounted on the underside of the roof panel and fitted with a turning handle to control the rate of air flow. The plastic handle, which was ivory for the Microbuses or black for other models, was fitted on the left-hand side of the air box.

Although never made by the Volkswagen factory, a number of specialist manufacturers supplied flower vases in ceramic, metal and glass specifically for fitting to both Transporter and Beetle dashboards. Some were beautifully hand-painted and thousands of owners fitted them. Today, original items are relatively rare and expensive whereas reproductions, which are every bit as good, are readily available and expensive. As powerful symbols of the spirit of the 1960s, Transporters of all kinds do not really look right without fresh flowers neatly blooming from a small vase.

Seen on a 1953 Panelvan, door interior panels and cab headlining are in fibre-board. Opening quarterlights, here to post-December 1952 pattern with 'lever' catch and swivelling mechanism roughly central top and bottom, helped to ventilate the otherwise poorly aired cab, and sliding side windows reduced production costs.

INSTRUMENTS & CONTROLS

Climbing into the cab of an early Transporter was always and remains a personal delight. Not because it is a 'driver's car', but because of the simplicity of the overall layout. It is a satisfying place to be, although not especially comfortable. The most imposing feature is the steering wheel, a delightful and beauti-fully made piece that would not look out of place on a pre-war racing car.

The thin-rimmed, three-spoke steering wheel

normal operating temperature, it stands to reason that the air-cooled engine is very hot and, via the exhaust system, the air which passes over the engine is at an equally high temperature. So, all things being equal, this hot air should adequately heat the cabin. And it does. But the criticism continues. Genuine Volks-wagen exhaust systems, which are responsible for

used until 1955 was to exactly the same design as the one fitted to early Beetles, but a little larger in diameter. The three spokes were hewn from slim but sturdy spindles of steel, and there was a horn button and chromed bezel at the centre of the hub. This wheel came in two colours, ivory (Microbus de luxe only) or black, the latter tending to fade with age and use to a wonderful tobacco colour. Steering wheel rims last seemingly for ever, although the nature of these vehicles dictated that they were subjected to extremes of wear and tear. The underside of the rim had finger grips around the circumference, although, for the most part, Volkswagen need not have incorporated them as most tradesmen in this period steered with one hand, the other being employed almost exclusively for holding and lighting cigarettes.

In March 1955, that significant Transporter watershed date, the lovely old three-spoker was replaced by a more modern two-spoke plastic item, also in black or ivory, which remained in use until the end of Splittie production in 1967. From a steering point of view, of course, the new wheel made no difference, but aesthetically it appeared to be a deliberate attempt to disregard real style. And for no other reason than to appease the whims of a larger world-wide audience,

an outrageous concept, especially for Volkswagen, who until this time had taken little notice of what customers wanted in the way of style. The two-spoker has finger grips on its underside and small ridges running down the outside of the two spokes. The central horn perimeter, which was always colour-matched to the wheel, contains a chromed ring and a black horn push. As previously and unlike the Beetle, there was no Wolfsburg crest in the centre except on the Microbus de luxe.

As launched, the Transporter did not have a dashboard as such, making do with a simple binnacle in front of the driver to house the speedometer. When the Microbus de luxe was introduced in June 1951, this model received a full-width dashboard. This basically comprised a single pressing with a pair of matching binnacles in front of driver and passenger, plus a further section between. In March 1955, all models received a full-width dashboard of completely new design, with a different instrument binnacle in front of the driver, a vertically ribbed surface across the rest of the width, and a full-width shelf below.

From the beginning of production, the Microbus de luxe had an ashtray with a lift-up chromed lid in the top of the full-width dashboard close to the

Microbus in extremely rare early form, dating from January 1951. Its interior is distinguishable from the less well appointed Kombi by full-length cloth headlining, matching material around windows, and fibreboard panelling below waist level. On Microbus only bench seats are upholstered in piped and fluted vinyl; ventilation is aided by opening rear side windows. Although the rear window is a later addition (for visibility!), the partitioned luggage compartment with vertical sliding shutter is an incredibly rare original feature.

Partition between cab and passenger area is fitted with two grab handles, the one on the right to aid entry; an ashtray sits below the horizontal grab handle. Dashboard centre section is a home-made addition. Side doors are also trimmed on the Microbus, and opened by a stout chromed handle that pushes downwards.

Early Microbus details: close-up of chromed finger latch for cab door sliding windows; first type of quarterlight, hinged at leading edge and with 'scissor' action catch; one of the pair of metal coathooks, typically engineered to last forever; spherical ashtray with sliding top; interior courtesy light in passenger compartment, manually operated with a chromed toggle switch.

division between the windscreen halves. When all the other models were fitted with the revised full-width dashboard, they received a less attractive ashtray with the lid now finished in body colour (or chrome for the Microbus de luxe). The early Microbus de luxe also had a large, circular clock on the passenger's side of the dashboard, but a smaller, rectangular clock was substituted after March 1955. The space in the middle of either design of full-width dashboard was intended for a radio, which was always an extra-cost option and usually a Blaupunkt or Telefunken. A small oval-shaped rear-view mirror was attached with two Phillips screws to the top of the windscreen division. The rear of the mirror is polished alloy and the bracket to which it is attached is chrome-plated.

Before March 1955 the speedometer was set in a panel painted matt black (or ivory on the Microbus de luxe) but the binnacle itself was painted body colour. Made by VDO, the original speedometer had a black face with white characters, and gear-change

points were highlighted in red. A delightfully simple instrument, crystal clear and similar to those fitted to early Beetles, it was calibrated to 80kph or 50mph, and its most charming feature is that the needle rotates 'backwards'. This design was abandoned in December 1953, the new speedometer having markings to 100kph or 70mph and a needle that turns in the conventional direction, a change that coincided with a rise in engine power from 25bhp to 30bhp.

Warning lights on pre-March 1955 vehicles are on the panel surrounding the speedometer. On the left is a red one at the top for the semaphore indicators and a blue one below for headlamp main beam. On the right is a red one at the top for ignition and a green one below for oil pressure. Two large switches are also fitted left and right, respectively for wipers and headlamps. The ignition switch sits between these two below the speedometer, with the separate starter button on the left-hand side of the binnacle. On top of the binnacle – or the full-width dashboard on the

Compared with earliest
Microbus, interior views of
1954 '23-window' Samba
show many differences – and
additional glass made for a
light and airy cabin. Note
standard three-seater central
bench with door-side folding
backrest, ivory-painted grab
handles on seat backs and
partition, revised trim with
armrests, longer grab handle
and plated ashtray on
partition, carpeted luggage
platform with chromed
restraining rails and rubbing
strips, and revised catch for
opening side window.

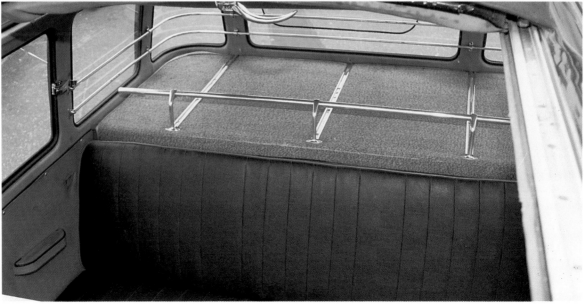

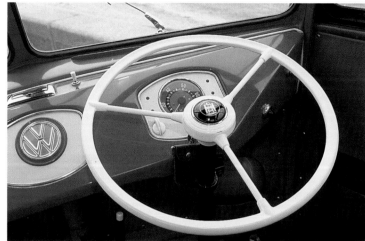

Microbus de luxe – is a toggle switch to operate the semaphore indicators.

With the arrival of the new dashboard in March 1955, the speedometer became a more modern-looking unit with warning lights incorporated, and other switchgear changes were made at the same time. The wiper and headlamp switches were transferred to the dashboard (respectively on the left and right of the steering column), the separate ignition switch and starter button was replaced by a combined ignition/starter switch fitted to the right-hand side of the instrument binnacle, and the toggle-operated semaphore switch was abandoned in favour of a slim stalk on the left-hand side of the steering column. This stalk is short and elegant, and has a plastic knob in either black or ivory on the end; the indicators were not of the self-cancelling breed until September 1957.

The post-March 1955 style of full-width dashboard remained fundamentally unchanged until the end of Split-screen production, an incredibly long

time by any standards and inconceivable for any manufacturer except Volkswagen. One detail did change, however, as the upper corners of the speedometer binnacle received rather more rounded corners – in the interests of safety – in July 1961.

One instrument that was conspicuous by its absence until 1961, and one which owners longed to be fitted, was a fuel gauge. Surprisingly, early Beetles and Porsche 356s also lacked this important dial, which is why many customers fitted after-market items. After Volkswagen decided to include a fuel gauge as standard, many owners updated their old models by fitting one retrospectively. Ambulances were an exception, incidentally, having had a fuel gauge since their introduction in December 1951.

Made by VDO, the standard fuel gauge is circular with a chromed bezel, and positioned outboard of the speedometer. In keeping with the speedometer, the gauge had a black face and white characters. Previously there had been no way of knowing how much

Normal pre-1955 full-width metal dashboard style, used as standard only on Microbus de luxe and painted body colour. Details show revised speedometer (post-December 1953) with conventional needle and calibration to 100kph or 70mph, chromed ashtray next to semaphore toggle switch, Count of Schulenberg's 'Wolfsburg Castle' crest on steering wheel (reserved for Microbus de luxe), and pre-1955 large circular clock. The standard VW roundel on the central panel could be replaced by an optional radio.

Kombi passenger compartment – this is a 1955 US School Bus – is more spartan and designed to be adaptable for load-carrying. Removable seats, secured to the floor by wing nuts, have exposed legs and vinyl trim without pleats or piping, while cabin walls and doors are untrimmed. Views through front passenger door and tailgate show rare option of two single seats in the cab with gap between and 'walk-through' partition behind.

Revised full-width dashboard came for all models in March 1955, along with less attractive two-spoke steering wheel, deletion of passenger-side grab handle, column stalk for indicators, new speedometer with inset warning lamps, and binnacle-mounted ignition/starter switch. This vehicle, a 1956 Panelvan, has optional opening 'Safari' screens, and ashtray is to painted 'non-Microbus de luxe' style.

At the same time as the new dashboard was introduced, cab ventilation was provided by an air distribution box on the underside of the roof, drawing air through new external vents above the split windscreen; this airbox has an optional control (the forward one) for the so-called 'ambulance fan', an additional fan fitted as standard only to Type 27s. Note that headlining was in fibreboard on all models except the Microbus, and fibreboard sun visor design differs from later vehicles. With seats removed, 1956 Panelvan cab shows spare wheel's revised position in a purpose-designed well; it was above the engine until March 1955.

fuel was in the tank, which is why there was a reserve fuel tank holding one gallon, the system being operated by a handle under the fuel tank on 'Barndoors' and by a push-pull knob in the middle of the cab floor after March 1955.

Rising from the floor in the centre of the cab, the straight gear lever was topped by a largish plain black or ivory-coloured knob. Because of its length, changing gear always felt odd, especially for those who were used to driving cars with a stubby lever and a narrow 'gate'. With the Transporter each gear position feels metres apart and there is also a fair bit of play, making it seem as if neutral is always selected.

Behind the gear lever are three further controls – or just one after July 1961 – mounted below the seats roughly in the centre of the cab and operating cables that run in conduits close to the centre of the chassis. Two small circular push-pull knobs for manual choke and reserve fuel tank are the controls which disap-

peared in July 1961, while the other is a much larger rotary heater knob. This has finger grips around its perimeter and, like the other two knobs, comes either in black or ivory-coloured plastic. The heater knob has the letters A (*Auf* for open) and Z (*Zu* for closed) highlighted in reverse colours. Whereas the Beetle's

Double-cab Pick-up front interior from February 1961 shows revised bench seat in plain vinyl, with extra shape for backrest. Aura of austerity continues in rear compartment with fibreboard headlining, fibreboard panelling almost to window height, ribbed rubber floor mat and bench seat again in plain vinyl – but Volkswagen, practical as ever, provided extra storage space below and behind the seat.

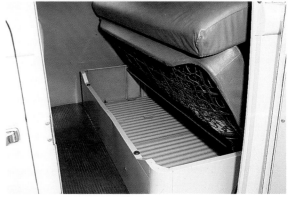

rotary heater knob was changed in August 1964 for lift-up handles, the Transporter's remained unaltered throughout Splittie production.

The handbrake lever is positioned in front of the gear lever and rises vertically from the floor. It was normally painted black and fitted with a black release button, but white paint with an ivory-coloured button was a nicety for the Microbus de luxe.

The foot pedals are bottom-hinged and rise from the floor like the Beetle's. Both the brake and clutch pedals are square and fitted with ribbed black rubber pads, whereas the first type of accelerator pedal is oddly shaped, a little like a beaver's tail, and was originally without a rubber pad. Although perfectly comfortable to use, this accelerator pedal was changed in March 1955 for a more conventional, flat, rectangular pedal. The foot-operated dipswitch that was fitted until August 1965, when this function was integrated into the indicator stalk, sits to the left of the clutch pedal. Clutch and accelerator cables run in separate conduits up the centre of the chassis.

Whereas the Beetle's bottom-hinged pedals were much criticised by journalists, although seasoned owners found them to be perfectly natural, they were just about bang on for the Transporter because the sit-

up-and-beg driving position lent itself well to the overall pedal layout. It is hardly surprising that contemporary road tests contain so little comment about the instruments and controls; there was very little to write about. 'Although austere, the instrument panel equipment is adequate for a van,' wrote Laurence Cotton in *Commercial* magazine in 1954.

Most writers who tested the Transporter tended to concentrate on the versatility of the vehicle and its practical advantages, although *Motor* in its May 1964 test commented: 'The driving position was relaxed and comfortable, but the floor-mounted gear lever and handbrake are a long reach away from tall people. All the controls are light and positive, though the steering at low speeds and over bad surfaces feels vague and spongey until you get used to it.'

Companies all over the world made various accessories for Transporters and Beetles, so it is not unusual to find all sorts of gauges adorning the dashboard. Some have been professionally fitted and a casual observer could quite easily be fooled into thinking that they are original Volkswagen fitments, but oil temperature gauges, tachometers and the rest were never fitted by the factory. And, if you discover a Transporter with a water temperature gauge, it might be as well to test the temperature of its owner.

ELECTRICS

Until August 1966 the Transporter was fitted with a Bosch six-volt battery housed inside the right-hand rear quarter panel, to the right of the engine. Of all the jokes made about air-cooled Volkswagens, even by folk who love them, it is this six-volt battery and the system it runs that has come in for more stick than anything else.

While in good order and all six volts are present and correct, the system works as well as any, but there are occasions – frosty, cold mornings when you are

Driver comfort was improved considerably with adjustable separate seat introduced as standard for 1963 model year. By this stage there is a passenger grab handle on dashboard and heater vents in footwells. Note that gear lever has an extension, a popular accessory with Beetle and Transporter owners alike.

It took Volkswagen 11 years from start of production to get round to fitting a fuel gauge – a circular VDO unit – and owners welcomed it with open arms. At bottom right, introduced in August 1964, is black plastic 'bellows' lid for pneumatic operation of plastic windscreen washer bottle.

Seen on a 1966 Samba, dashboard remained little changed in latter years of Split-screen production. Steering wheel continued to have Wolfsburg crest on horn button for this top-of-range model, but design is different from that seen earlier on 1954 Samba.

late for work – when three or four of those precious volts go AWOL and, as is well known, the remaining two or three are rarely sufficient to fire the headlamps into action let alone churn the starter motor into life. Which is why so many owners have converted their vehicles to 12-volt systems.

As six-volt components are now becoming increasingly rare – and even batteries are becoming difficult to obtain – changing to 12 volts may be a more sensible approach for anyone considering major restoration work. Volkswagen offered 12-volt conversions to special order – mainly for the benefit of

doctors and nurses in Britain – long before they were standardised in August 1966, so changing a pre-1966 vehicle to the more modern system is not necessarily going against the grain of factory originality.

Virtually all of the electrical components were made by Bosch, but the semaphore indicators were supplied by SWF. The semaphores were made in left- and right-hand pairs and are operated by solenoids. The lenses were originally ribbed, but smooth ones were fitted from early 1953. Made by SWF, the simple windscreen motor is housed behind the front body panel and drives a simple linkage to the wiper arms,

Close-ups show speedometer (now calibrated to 120kph or 80mph, and housed in a pod with rounded upper corners) and Microbus de luxe standard-fitment clock (post-1955 rectangular style).

Front and rear compartments of 1966 Samba. Note late-production two-tone seat trim (with 'chequered' effect for wearing surfaces), door and cabin wall panelling with contrast centre sections bordered by bright trim strips, and partition intrusion (with shelf above) to accommodate spare wheel.

which were rather short and also made by SWF; a stronger wiper motor was fitted from March 1955.

The 0.5hp starter motor, flange-mounted on the right-hand side of the gearbox, was fitted with a sole-noid and there was an outrigger bush in the body of the gearbox for supporting the armature shaft. In August 1966, the nine-tooth starter pinion was altered – and the motor itself uprated to 0.7hp – because the change to 12-volt electrics necessitated fitting a larger flywheel, which has a ring gear with 130 teeth instead of the original 109. At the same time the bore of the outrigger bush was reduced from 12.5mm to 10.89mm.

Not all starter motors were made by Bosch, a good few having been made by Volkswagen, but official records do not specify which models were fitted with which type. It appears, however, that Volkswagen-made units predominated after March 1955. In prin-ciple the two types are identical, but the Volkswagen ones have slightly modified solenoid and pinion assemblies. The differences are best appreciated by referring to the Volkswagen workshop manual.

The dynamo, which sits on top of the purpose-built cast alloy pedestal bolted to the right half of the engine crankcase, has an alloy body and is belt-driven from the pulley bolted to the crankshaft. It is secured to the pedestal with a metal strap. In turn, the engine's cooling fan is driven by the dynamo's armature shaft, which is carried in ball bearings, drive being taken off the front of the dynamo. A regulator with a built-in cut-out sits on top of the body of the dynamo.

Originally the dynamo delivered 130 watts at around 2500rpm, but a number of vehicles – exactly how many is not known – were fitted with 160-watt dynamos during October 1953 before the more powerful unit was standardised from December of the same year. In June 1959 the dynamo was uprated again, to 180 watts – not that the headlamps shone discernibly brighter as a result. Both Bosch and Volks-wagen dynamos were fitted, the Volkswagen units generally appearing after March 1955, but the two are very similar in design and, again, the minute differ-ences between them are best appreciated by referring to a Volkswagen workshop manual.

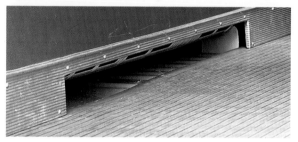

The Bosch single-tone horn is fitted on a bracket under the left-hand front wing and should just about last for ever. However, some have been known to give up the ghost and, along with so many six-volt items, genuine replacements are not easy to come by.

Bolted via a U bracket to the left-hand side of the engine's fan housing, the coil has a black body and produces in the region of 8-9000 sparks per second, which was seemingly not sufficient for the majority of people who, at the slightest hint of the coil 'breaking down', rushed off to replace the original item with a Blue Bosch coil, a superior piece of equipment producing in the region of 12,000 sparks per second. The Blue coils are now so popular that the majority of Transporters, and Beetles for that matter, have them fitted. Few concours judges find them acceptable, however, and you will normally lose points in a beauty contest for having one installed.

Like the starter motor and dynamo, the original distributor was made by Bosch, but a switch was made to a Volkswagen-made item in March 1955, although not in all cases. Early distributors were Bosch VJR/4BR/25 or VW 211/905/205H items, while post-1959 1200s and the later 1500s had either a Bosch ZV/PAU/4R/5mk or a VW 113/905/205B – but most vehicles use Bosch rather than VW distributors. Ignition timing for all Transporters should be set at 10 degrees BTDC. To begin with the distributor had a centrifugal advance mechanism. From 1955 it also incorporated a vacuum control as well, but from February 1959 there was vacuum control only. When adjusting the contact breaker points, the gap should measure 0.16in with the breaker arm on the highest point of the cam.

All four plug leads throughout production had copper wires and black plastic cables. Original specification replacements continue to be available, but the non-original silicon type, which usually have coloured plastic covers, have a tendency to build up resistance to current and, therefore, a relatively short life. To keep them out of harm's way, the plug leads were held in place with a conduit near the fan housing, but after May 1959 the conduit was changed for plastic fasteners clipped to the fan housing.

As a rule, Transporters were supplied with Bosch sparking plugs, but the factory recommended a number of different types – Bosch W226 T1, Beru K225/14u2, Lodge H14 or HN, Champion L10A, AC43L, Auto-Lite AE6, AER6 and KLG F70. Today, it would seem that choice comes down to whatever you can get your hands on. A recent visit to my local motor accessory shop for a new set of plugs produced a smile on the face of the proprietor and a polite explanation that delivery would take approximately three weeks.

Compared with earlier Samba, rear interior views of 1966 version show individual grab handles for central bench, headlining in perforated vinyl (standard from September 1964), carpeted luggage platform that lacks rubbing strips and is lower owing to spare wheel's revised location behind front seats, and heater outlet below rear bench.

Housed on the right-hand side of the engine compartment, the Bosch six-volt battery has a black-painted metal cover and is secured by a metal strap.

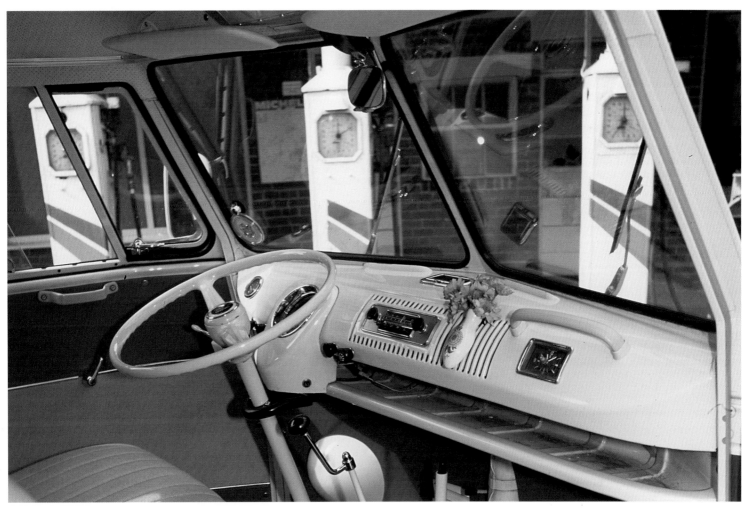

Interior of this 1967 Splittie is particularly cheery, with bright colour scheme and dashboard-mounted flower vase. Note black knobs for lights/wipers/radio unique to the last model year, post-August 1961 padded sun visors, and after-market gear lever extension. Seat pleating, just visible, is not original.

The electrode gap should be set at 0.024–0.028in and the plugs should be changed at 3000-mile intervals as part of general servicing. Modern spark plugs will last a good deal longer but, beyond 9000 miles, fuel consumption tends to suffer. The switch for the oil pressure light is housed at the back of the engine at the rear of the oil gallery, which leads from the oil pump itself to the oil cooler situated on top of the left-hand side of the crankcase.

The Transporter's lighting system is generally very reliable as all the cables are protected by plastic covers, faults developing usually because of corroded or otherwise faulty connectors. Power output of the lamp bulbs in watts are as follows: headlamps, 45/40; parking, 4; stop and tail, 20/5; registration number plate, 10; interior courtesy light, 5; indicators, 18; instrument and dashboard warning lights, 1.2. Fuses for the electrical system are situated on the rear of the dashboard, with a further set for the headlamps next to the fuel tank. From 1960 there were eight fuses instead of six located under the dashboard.

Press criticism about the quite dreadful headlamps was again conspicuous by its absence, due, one can assume, to road tests being carried out solely during the hours of daylight. Had journalists actually taken the trouble to drive at night, it is probable that the switch to 12-volt electrics would have occurred sooner than August 1966 – although Volkswagen was not noted for responding quickly to criticism, constructive or otherwise.

The 12-volt system was exactly the same in principle as the six-volter except that the components were uprated, as previously described in the case of the Volkswagen 0.7hp starter motor and the 130-tooth flywheel ring gear. Some, but not all, lamp bulbs became more powerful, ratings in watts being as follows: headlamps, 45/40; sealed-beam headlamps fitted to American-spec vehicles (from 1960), 50/40; indicators, 21; stop and tail, 21/5; registration number plate, 10; interior courtesy light, 5; parking light, 4; instrument and dashboard warning lights, 2.

For most owners – not purists, of course – the 12-volt electrical system came almost as a gift from Heaven. The 12-volt starter motor has a tendency to spin many more times than the six-volt item before the engine fires into life, but it always gets there in the end, even on the coldest mornings. And the 12-volt headlamps were a great advantage, of course, although they are still rather feeble by modern standards.

Along with the introduction of 12-volt electrics, Volkswagen scrapped the irritating two-key system and provided just one key for locks and ignition.

ENGINE

If there is any justification for describing any power unit as a 'classic', the famous air-cooled, horizontally-opposed, four-cylinder, Porsche-designed engine must be regarded as the classic among classics. Rugged, durable and reliable for thousands of miles if maintained properly, the Volkswagen engine has powered Beetles, Transporters, Porsches and light aircraft, and has seen service in many factories throughout the world in industrial applications. Widely misunderstood and perceived by many to be an intricate complex of unfathomable metal, the secret of this engine's success is undoubtedly in its simplicity and, of course, it remains in production today in Mexico.

The engine is the same as the one fitted to the Beetle and, in its original guise, produced a maximum 25bhp at 3300rpm from 1131cc (69.02cu in). Bore and stroke measure 75mm × 64mm (2.95in × 2.52in), and the compression ratio is a low 5.8:1 to take account of wide variations in fuel quality that existed throughout Europe. The lack of reliability that dogged the first production Beetles in 1945 was cured early on, which is why this almost unbelievably under-stressed unit is often said to be Volkswagen's most reliable engine ever, several examples having recorded well over 300,000 miles without apparent fatigue.

It is a light and compact unit – a strong, fit person could just about pick one up unaided – and almost every aspect of it is unconventional. Made of light alloy, the two-piece crankcase is split vertically on the centre line through the main bearings and bolted together. There is no sump in the accepted sense, the oil draining to the bottom of the crankcase when the engine is switched off. For the purpose of changing

On 'Barndoor' models, Beetle power unit with integrally cast dynamo pedestal is externally identical in 1131cc 25bhp or 1192cc 30bhp forms; the change occurred in December 1953. Cavernous engine bay also contains fuel tank, filler neck and horizontally mounted spare wheel. Note wonderful simplicity of oil bath air cleaner on top of single Solex carburettor.

Starting handle, discontinued during the 1959 model year, was a hangover from vintage days and not strictly necessary, but came in useful when six-volt battery suffered dreaded voltage drop.

Fuel filler cap, seen on a 'Barndoor', was stamped with VW motif; neck of 80mm width is sufficiently large to allow access to the tank by hand!

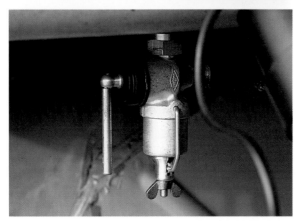

Without the benefit of a fuel gauge, early Transporters had a reserve of one gallon (5 litres) operated by a tap below the tank.

the oil, there is a circular strainer plate on the underside of the crankcase which simply unbolts.

Eight long studs threaded into the crankcase halves hold the finned, cast iron cylinder barrels and light alloy cylinder heads (mated to each other without gaskets) by passing directly through them, the heads being secured on the outer ends of the studs by nuts. The separate cylinder barrels, which were coated with heat-resistant black paint to prevent premature rusting, are seated in circular holes cast into the two crankcase halves.

The combustion chambers are roughly to a hemispherical design, and breathing, which was intentionally restricted in the interests of safety and longevity, was through horizontally disposed inlet and exhaust valves of 28.6mm (1.05in) diameter. The short crankshaft runs in three main thin-wall bearings – steel-backed with copper-lead inserts – and one additional

bearing that acts as a support for the auxiliary drives. Mounted below the crankshaft and driven from it by helical gears, the camshaft, which until August 1965 was mounted in the crankcase without bearings, operates the overhead valves via rocker arms and pushrods, each cam operating two rods.

The pushrods are drilled with small holes at each end to provide lubrication to the rocker arms, and are contained within the pushrod tubes, which are sealed at both ends with rubber washers. These seals are notoriously prone to wear and occasionally allow copious quantities of oil to leak out as a result. Made by Mahle, the flat-topped alloy pistons are secured to the conventional, forged connecting rods with a floating gudgeon pin that is held in place with a circlip. Each piston is fitted with two compression rings and one oil control ring. The connecting rods are fitted with high-tensile bolts screwed into the lower caps. The thin-wall big-end bearings are steel-backed copper-lead with white metal.

Bolted to the top of the crankcase is the vertically-mounted, black-painted, sheet-steel fan housing. This contains two major components: the oil cooler (also painted black) on the left-hand side and the cooling fan on the right. The cooling fan itself consists of a rotor mounted on the nose of the dynamo armature shaft and is driven at twice engine speed by the fan belt at the other end. Cooling air is drawn from outside through louvres in the outer bodywork, and the fan blows it over the oil cooler, cylinder barrels and heads.

Black-painted steel ducting trays – commonly referred to as 'tinware' – are fitted over the cylinder heads and barrels to prevent heat produced by the engine escaping into the engine bay and causing overheating. A black rubber seal around the perimeter of the engine compartment plays a vital role in creating an air-tight seal between the tinware and bodywork. Hot 'spent' air is expelled at the rear of the vehicle below the valance, but is also utilised by the heater boxes at the front of the exhaust system for heating the cabin.

The main problem with this method of cabin heating was that, when the engine picked up mud from the road and became encrusted with oil in old age, the hot air passing over the engine would pick up rather unpleasant fumes, making life uncomfortable for passengers. This is why the heater boxes were changed for heat exchangers in August 1963. With this new arrangement, the exhaust pipes were encased inside roughly cylindrical metal chambers, so that hot air from the exhaust and engine never went near a dirty surface.

Initially a Type 26VFI or VFJ downdraught Solex carburettor was fitted, but this was changed for a Solex 28PCI from October 1952. Made of aluminium alloy, the carburettor comprises a body and float chamber, and is topped by a domed metal oil bath air filter with a detachable lid held in place by spring clips. Fuel is

dispensed to the cylinder heads through a long, small-bore inlet manifold. Made of steel and painted grey, this manifold branches from a single pipe into two directly below the carburettor. Each pipe is bolted to the top surface of the cylinder heads and feeds the fuel/air mixture into a single port in each head.

The exceptional length of this inlet manifold was a distinct disadvantage in cold weather. Because the fuel/air mixture has such a long way to travel, low external temperatures can cause icing. From the very beginning Volkswagen recognised this tendency and fitted 'pre-heat' pipes to take warm air from the exhaust area to the carburettor stem. A more efficient system, accomplished by running a pipe from the right-hand heat exchanger to the air filter, was introduced in May 1959, but still did not completely solve the perennial problems of icing.

Engine oil, all 4½ pints (2.5 litres) of it, is drawn from the bottom of the crankcase through a gear-type oil pump situated in the rear of the crankcase and driven by the camshaft. Oil is pushed through holes in the case to the crankshaft, camshaft and pushrods. Oilways are also drilled into the crankshaft to connect the main journals with the big-end bearings. Naturally, an air-cooled engine relies just as much on oil as it does on air to keep it operating at the correct temperature, and conventional wisdom dictates that a monograde is preferable to a modern multi-grade, but

thousands of owners switched to the latter years ago without any apparent harm to their engines.

With just 25bhp on tap, the early Transporters were not exactly flying machines. With a full load on board they fairly struggled up steep hills, and fuel consumption suffered as well. The true top speed of the Panelvan was around 55mph (86kph) with acceleration between 25-50mph (40-80kph) taking 80sec with a full load. This was slow – although not excessively so by contemporary standards – but Volkswagen invested heavily in making improvements as it became more profitable. Three years into production moves were made to increase power output.

In December 1953 the new 30bhp engine was announced. To the same design as the original, it differed in a few comparatively minor details. The capacity was increased to 1192cc (72.74cu in) by increasing the bore from 75mm (2.95in) to 77mm (3.03in). At 64mm (2.52in) the stroke remained unchanged, but the compression ratio was raised to 6.6:1, trough-shaped piston crowns were fitted and the inlet valves were increased in diameter from 28.6mm (1.05in) to 30mm (1.18in). However, in August of the same year, the pistons reverted to the flat-top type. Maximum power of 30bhp was produced at 3400rpm and torque went up from 67Nm at 2000rpm to 76Nm at 2000rpm.

Volkswagen was never in the habit of exaggerating

In essence, robust 1192cc 30bhp engine remained unchanged until May 1959, but oil bath air cleaner was moved to the left when engine bay was reduced in height, in March 1955.

From May 1959 dynamo pedestal was made detachable and compression ratio was raised from 6.1:1 to 6.6:1. Ratio increased again, to 7:1, in June 1960 with introduction of 34bhp version of 1192cc engine.

performance figures, always straying on the side of caution in its beautifully produced and illustrated sales literature. As *Road & Track* commented in its Microbus test in December 1956: 'The factory provides a warning sign in front of the driver which reads, "The allowable top speed of this vehicle is 50 miles per hour." No-one pays much attention to this, or for that matter, the rev limit marks... Any Kombi, Microbus or Camper owner will tell you this figure is absurd – he has indicated 70mph on a dead level highway for hours at a time.'

The increase in power was welcomed by Volkswagen's loyal clientele, and sales rose significantly. An increase of 5bhp does not sound much, but when you have only 25bhp to start with it makes a world of difference, especially when accelerating from rest.

After the move to the Hanover factory in 1956, Volkswagen's engineers awarded themselves something of a rest and engine modifications were few and far between, although some changes occurred at the March 1955 watershed date. The most visible one, required because the height of the engine bay was reduced, was the use of a different air filter. Instead of the small, domed unit fitted previously, the much more familiar one with a long intake pipe with the oil bath over to the left of the engine found its way into the engine bay. Another small but useful change was the reduction in size of the dynamo nut from 36mm

(1.42in) to 21mm (0.83in), which allowed the same tool to be used for changing the fan belt and sparking plugs. At the same time the Solex 28PCI carburettor was introduced and had a nylon float instead of the alloy one previously fitted.

From September 1957 the oil cooler was made shorter and, for extra strength, it was brazed rather than soldered. From February 1959 helicoil inserts were used in the cylinder heads for the sparking plug threads instead of threaded bushes as previously. However, this modification was already installed on approximately 65 per cent of total production from September 1958.

Towards the end of the 1950s, it became obvious that the 30bhp engine – good old slogger that it undoubtedly was – was becoming a little breathless and long in the tooth. More power was needed, but Volkswagen chose to ignore the obvious route. The German specialist tuning company, Okrasa (now Oettinger), had offered a simple tuning kit to uprate the little engine by producing twin-port cylinder heads, twin carburettors, a special exhaust system and larger cylinder barrels and pistons, which took the cubic capacity to 1.3 litres and power output to around 70bhp – more than double the output of the standard unit.

Curiously, Volkswagen would not accept that Okrasa's version was sufficiently durable for everyday use although, as it turns out, a well-maintained Okrasa is every bit as reliable and long-lived. So Nordhoff, as ever, stuck to his guns and in May 1959 the Transporter was fitted with a redesigned engine which, until June 1960, when power output was rated at 34bhp, was no more powerful than the previous unit.

To a casual observer the new engine was almost, but not quite, indistinguishable from the previous one, but many of its components were changed and improved. Again, this increase in power, small as it appears to be, was actually detectable from the driver's seat and welcomed by customers worldwide.

Although the capacity of 1192cc was retained with exactly the same bore and stroke as before, the cylinder heads were redesigned with wedge-shaped combustion chambers, separate cam followers and overhead valves arranged at a slant, and the compression ratio was raised to 7.0:1. Valve diameter also increased to 31mm (1.22in) inlet and 30.5m (1.20in) exhaust. The crankcase was more strongly made and had stronger studs and bolts, the cylinder barrels were spaced slightly further apart, the fuel pump drive was modified and the crankshaft was stronger.

Another small change was that the 40mm (1.57in) rear crankshaft bearing was made narrower and had a groove to prevent oil leaking past the bearing, the groove redirecting oil into a guide in the crankcase. In effect, this modification was made to stop the possibility of oil leaking through the centre of the crankshaft pulley. The valve timing was also changed from .004in to .008in for inlet and exhaust.

All of these modifications were under the skin, but the new engine is outwardly distinguishable from the 25bhp and 30bhp units by its alloy dynamo pedestal, which was detachable from the crankcase instead of being cast integrally with it as previously. The new dynamo pedestal was located on the right-hand side of the engine in the same position as previously and had four bolts to secure it. Instead of the engine number being stamped on the dynamo pedestal as previously, it now appeared on the crankcase immediately below the base of the pedestal.

Another distinct advantage of the new engine was that it became a little quieter, the speed of the cooling fan having been reduced by the use of a larger dynamo pulley and a smaller crankshaft pulley. As the engine in the Transporter was so far away from the cab, drivers never noticed a difference in engine clatter, but pedestrians did.

The author of *The Autocar*'s April 1960 test commented: 'Van engines usually share the front compartment with the driver and his passenger, and the noise level is consequently high. With the rear-engined Volkswagen, it was expected that the car would be quieter than its competitors, but even then the remarkably low level of noise came as a surprise. At tickover the engine is scarcely audible, and right through the rev range there is very little noise from it to worry the front occupants. Rear seat passengers hear more, but they are still impressed by the quietness. At any speed there is no indication that the car is being driven too hard, even when the engine is taken up to high revs in indirect gears.'

In June 1960 the power increase to 34bhp came when the Solex 28PCI carburettor was replaced by the 28PICT, which was fitted with a thermostatically-controlled automatic choke controlled by a bi-metallic spring, and heated by a heater element. To improve cold starting further, the left-hand heater box was modified so that a flexible card-type hose could be fitted to it, the purpose being to utilise warm air from the exhaust and direct it into the air cleaner. At the same time, the air cleaner was modified to include a weighted flap in order to feed the carburettor with warm air in cold weather. This went some way towards addressing the problem of carburettor icing, but did not eradicate it altogether.

At this time, Volkswagen's engineers and draughtsmen had been working at a feverish pitch. Both the Transporter and Beetle had been treated to dozens of modifications and, in a quest to find a replacement model for the ageing Beetle, the company launched a new car. The Type 3 saloon was not a great success by Volkswagen's normal standards, but the company must have been doing something right as in October 1962 it celebrated the production of its millionth Transporter, which had actually been built in the middle of the previous month.

Now in a new decade, one in which the developed world became increasingly affluent, Volkswagen went from strength to strength. In North America Ford and Chevrolet launched their versions of the Volkswagen Transporter with the Econoline and Greenbrier models respectively, and, of course, both were considerably bigger and more powerful. Volkswagen reacted immediately by offering the Type 3 saloon's 1500 engine for Transporters exported to the USA from January 1963. The 34bhp 1200 models continued to be sold alongside the 1500, but the vast majority of exports to North America were 1500s. By March 1963 all passenger-carrying Transporters sold elsewhere came with the option of the 1500 engine, and by August of the same year all models were available with this option. The 1200 engine was finally dropped from the range in October 1965.

As fitted to the Type 3 saloon, the cooling fan on the 1500 engine was mounted vertically on the nose of the crankshaft at the rear of the engine. As this arrangement was not suitable for the Transporter, Volkswagen resorted to the more conventional upright fan housing mounted vertically on top of the engine. With an increased bore and stroke of 83mm × 69mm (3.27in × 2.72in) capacity worked out at 1493cc (91.11cu in). With the compression ratio also higher at 7.5:1, the new engine produced a healthy – but still comparatively feeble – 42bhp at 3800rpm.

As a result of this extra power, the Transporter's payload went up from 750kg (¾ tonne) to 1000kg (1

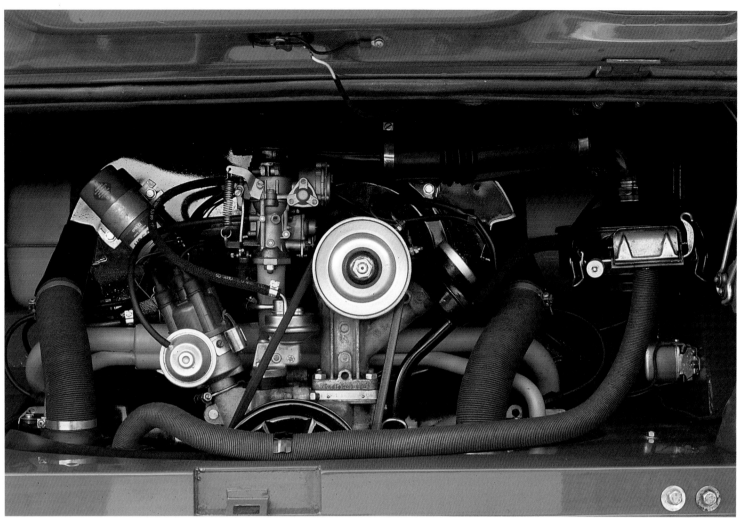

The more powerful 1500 engine introduced in March 1963, initially as an option, raised Transporter's top speed to 65mph, which was considered so potentially dangerous that a carburettor governor was fitted from August 1964. The 1500's air cleaner and hose arrangement is very different.

tonne), and the safe top speed was quoted at 65mph (105kph), although the majority of owners ignored factory advice as usual. So, from August 1964 a governor was fitted to the carburettor to limit the possibility of a vehicle becoming dangerously out of control at high speed with a full load on board.

At first rather small diameter valves – 31.5mm (1.24in) inlets and 30mm (1.18in) exhausts – were fitted. To improve engine breathing, larger valves were fitted from August 1965, the inlets being increased to 35.5mm (1.40in) and the exhausts to 32mm (1.26in), which led to an increase in power output from 42bhp to 44bhp at 4000rpm. Early 1500 Transporters were fitted with the 34bhp 1200's Solex 28 PICT carburettor, but the more powerful version of the 1500 engine had the revised 28 PICT-1. The settings for the pre-June 1960 28 PCI, post-June 1960 28 PICT and post-August 1965 28 PICT-1 are as follows:

VENTURI

1200 (28 PCI)	21.5mm
1200 and 1500 (28 PICT)	22.5mm

MAIN JET

1200 (28 PCI)	117.5mm
1500 (28 PICT)	115mm

AIR CORRECTION JET

1200 (28 PCI)	180
1200 and 1500 (28 PICT)	145Y

Even if its output was still modest, the new engine was appreciably more powerful than the 34bhp 1200 engine. In 1963 *Hot Rod Special* commented: 'While it has substantial differences from the older model, the primary one with which we are concerned is its increased power, something that the wagon has needed since its introduction. With the early engine top speed was about 60mph, and it was not uncommon to pull modest grades in third gear, flat out at 35mph with only a medium load. Granted, the enforced speed reduction often came as a welcome period of relaxation during a long trip, but it was likewise frustrating to see domestic autos zipping past at 65. The added power has not completely solved the problem, but it has been alleviated.'

Most contemporary road testers tended to avoid commenting on the new engine, concentrating more on the detail equipment supplied in the specialist-produced Camper versions. However, the May 1967 issue of *Motor* commented on the 'surprisingly good fuel consumption figure of 29.2mpg', which its author attributed to the engine governing device preventing the throttle being opened sufficiently to produce peak engine speeds. Several owners actually removed the carburettor governor because, as the same *Motor* road test observed, 'In practice, the governor can be an embarrassment when it causes a sudden cessation of power build-up when passing another vehicle in an intermediate gear.'

Overall the 1500 engine as fitted to the Transporter, Beetle and Type 3 was arguably Volkswagen's finest air-cooled power unit, because it more or less combined the reliability of the 1200 with the power of the later 1600 in one exceptionally strong and durable engine. Maintained and used properly, these engines will easily last 200,000 miles and more. It is the classic Volkswagen engine – the 1600 unit fitted to the first of the post-1967 Bay-window models was altogether different.

TRANSMISSION

Acknowledged as being one of the best gearboxes of its time, the Porsche-designed Transporter unit is located between the rear of the chassis and the engine. It is fairly unconventional and highly complex in design, and rebuilding one, which requires special tools, is a task for experienced mechanics.

At its front mounting to the chassis, the gearbox is protected from engine torque and vibration by a rubber damper, and the gear change rod leads through the front of the alloy casing. At the rear the gearbox is bolted directly to the engine with four bolts, the removal of which is virtually all it takes to extract the engine through the rear of the vehicle.

The rear of the gearbox casing is also protected from vibration and engine torque by two sturdy rubber mountings which bolt to a transverse metal cradle attached to two longitudinal and roughly parallel members, referred to in Volkswagen lore as the 'fork' and welded to the rear of the chassis. Split vertically and longitudinally, the ribbed, alloy-cased gearbox and final drive assembly are integrated into one compact and rigid unit.

The gearbox is driven from the engine by an input shaft and a Fichtel & Sachs 180mm (7.1in) – or 200mm (7.9in) on the 1500 – single-plate dry clutch, which is splined to the input shaft. The two friction surfaces of the clutch are applied to the flywheel, which is bolted to what Volkswagen owners usually refer to as the front of the engine, and to the pressure plate fitted to the clutch cover. Positioned behind the centre line of the rear axle shafts, the clutch is operated by an adjustable cable and contained within the bellhousing of the gearbox.

When the clutch is operated, a thrust ring makes contact with the clutch release plate which, in turn, disengages the clutch plate from the flywheel. An integral part of the gearbox, the differential assembly comprises a differential housing with housing covers, side gears, pinions and pinion shafts, and solid driveshafts articulated with universal joints and contained within black-painted steel axle tubes. Both driveshafts are flattened on their inner ends and are fitted between fulcrum plates in the side gears.

The sliding nature of the axles in between the fulcrum plates, in conjunction with the rocking of the fulcrum plates in the side gears, allows the universal joints to work, a simple but exceptionally strong design which is almost, but not quite, unbreakable. Gearbox and final drive lubricant is protected from contamination by dirt by rubber boots clipped over the inner ends of the driveshafts. Threaded filler and drain plugs are located on the side and bottom of the casing respectively.

Utilising a wholly separate oil supply, reduction gearboxes are carried on the outer ends of the axle tubes, each box housing a pair of reduction gears. These were first used on the Porsche-designed Kübelwagens during the Second World War as an aid to acceleration in difficult ground conditions, or pulling away from rest with a heavy load on board. Although this system appears to be an unnecessary complication, it works well.

One journalist writing in the January 1955 issue of the American journal Mechanix commented: 'The Volkswagen will climb anything but not fast. When the grade gets real grim the Kombi's speed is not much better than a fast walk but it will get there… Patience is a European motoring trait, unknown over here. The average American driver would slit his throat if he had to go over the Alps in the average European low-powered family car. It's like walking upstairs pulling a bull moose. To the typical American, that underpowered, low speed, slow grind is similar to a nail scraping on a blackboard. In Europe it's the order of the day so no-one thinks anything about it.'

Made of cast iron, the reduction gearbox casings are in two pieces and bolted together. The inner casing is located by the driveshaft tube and the longitudinal trailing arm (known as a 'spring plate'), the latter being secured to it with four bolts. The inner casing also has an integral casting to which the shock absorber is attached. The oil filler plug is in the top of the casing and the drain plug is at the base. Volkswagen recommended the use of SAE 90 Hypoid oil, which should be changed every 30,000 miles. The outer casing has the brake drum back plate secured to it with four bolts.

Supported in ball bearings, the outer ends of the driveshafts are splined and carry the one-piece hubs and brake drums. The reduction gears are arranged vertically one on top of the other, the top ones being driven directly by the driveshafts from the gearbox.

In its original guise the gearbox was without synchromesh and some owners despised it, mainly through their inability to change up and down without crunching the gear wheels. From March 1953 all models had synchromesh on second, third and fourth gears, while an all-synchromesh 'box arrived in May 1959 and pre-dated the same modification to the Beetle by three months.

The all-synchromesh gearbox introduced in 1959 was in fact a wholly revised unit, and similar to the one fitted to the Porsche 356. Instead of using a two-piece case split vertically and longitudinally through the centre line, the casing – known as the tunnel type

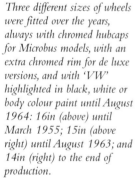

Three different sizes of wheels were fitted over the years, always with chromed hubcaps for Microbus models, with an extra chromed rim for de luxe versions, and with 'VW' highlighted in black, white or body colour paint until August 1964: 16in (above) until March 1955; 15in (above right) until August 1963; and 14in (right) to the end of production.

were modified. The number of teeth on the reduction gears was also increased from 21/15 to 25/18.

With the original configuration, the engine and gearbox have to be completely removed in order to change a driveshaft. With detachable side plates, the driveshafts can be removed with the gearbox in place. With the later gearbox, it is also possible to alter the shim or mesh adjustment on the pinion shaft without having to go to dismantle the pinion assembly.

The final change to the transmission came in August 1963 when the driveshafts were increased in diameter from 30mm (1.18in) to 35mm (1.38in), and supported on their outer ends by roller bearings instead of ball bearings.

By and large both the early and tunnel type gearboxes are just about bullet-proof, over-engineered to the point where they can accept power units of 150bhp without exploding.

WHEELS & TYRES

Transporter wheels were made of steel to the same basic five-bolt design as those fitted to contemporary Beetles, Porsche 356s and, oddly enough, Porsche tractors. The wheels were originally solid, but all models had four narrow slots between the rim and centre from March 1955 to August 1963. To begin with the wheels were of 16in diameter, but were reduced in size to 15in in March 1955 and to 14in in August 1963.

— was cast in one piece with detachable side plates to make servicing easier. At the same time the final drive was made 15mm lower, and the engine and gearbox assembly was tilted forwards by 2 degrees with the result that the front gearbox mounting, gear lever operating rod and the three gearbox selector shafts

Officially, most Transporter wheels were painted Silver White (L82), irrespective of model or trim level, but in reality they were often painted in body colour or two-tone schemes until the early 1960s, by the factory or by dealers. Today, it is common to find Microbuses in particular with two-tone wheels – some are even chromed – in a variety of combinations, one of which is usually body colour.

The domed hubcaps also differed on the two Microbus models in that they were always chromium-plated on the de luxe. In standard form, the other models had the same style hubcaps, but they were mostly painted Light Grey (L345), although Kombi owners could have chromed items as extra-cost options. In effect this option also applied to Panelvan and Pick-up owners, but few bothered. Alloy wheel trims were also standard on the Microbus de luxe.

The V-over-W emblem in the centre of the hubcaps was highlighted in a variety of colours, black being the most common, until 1963/64, when someone at Volkswagen – an accountant no doubt – finally twigged that Volkswagen could save a great deal of money on paint. This was a great pity, but many owners continued to highlight their V-over-W symbols using a brush and a small tin of enamel paint in a colour of their choice.

Throughout Splittie production the hubcaps were fitted to the wheels with spring clips attached to the wheels. Removing a hubcap was always a fairly unsubtle task which, before 12 January 1959, usually involved digging a screwdriver between the cap and the wheel, and banging around until it fell to the ground with a clank and inevitable damage to paint and chrome. After 1959, Volkswagen thoughtfully included a special puller in the tool kit which fitted into two small holes in the hubcaps. However, because the puller was so small and was not needed very often, most owners lost theirs and reverted to the crude screwdriver method – which is why original hubcap pullers are sought-after today.

The tyres fitted to all Split-screen Transporters were crossplies. The original 5.50×16 tyres were changed to 6.40×15 in 1955 and 7.00×14 in 1963. Most were supplied by Michelin and Continental. Original crossplies are becoming increasingly difficult to obtain these days and the majority of Transporter owners appear to have switched to radials – I applaud their decision.

In my experience – and I learned the hard way – every single crossply tyre designed to fit air-cooled Volkswagens should be flown in a large rocket to a distant galaxy in the hope that the whole lot disappears into a black hole en route. Crossplies wear out quickly, and give the most weird handling characteristics and inferior roadholding. In fact I can think of nothing to commend them. And where safety is concerned, preserving originality does not come into the equation if old Transporters are going to be used for their intended purpose.

All wheels had five-bolt fixings (left), regardless of diameter. To prevent damage to the hubcap by the traditional screwdriver method, a hubcap puller (below left) was supplied in the tool kit from January 1959.

GEAR RATIOS

Non-synchromesh gearbox, 1950-53 1st, 3.60:1; 2nd, 2.07:1; 3rd, 1.25:1; 4th, 0.80:1; reverse, 6.60:1
Gearbox with synchromesh on top three ratios, 1953-59 1st, 3.60:1; 2nd, 1.88:1; 3rd, 1.23:1; 4th, 0.82:1; reverse, 4.63:1
30bhp gearbox, from May 1959 1st, 3.80:1; 2nd, 2.06:1; 3rd, 1.32:1; 4th, 0.89:1; reverse, 3.88:1
34/42/44bhp gearbox, from June 1960 1st, 3.80:1; 2nd, 2.06:1; 3rd, 1.22:1; 4th, 0.82:1; reverse, 3.88:1
1500 gearbox 1st, 3.80:1; 2nd, 2.06:1; 3rd, 1.26:1; 4th, 0.82:1; reverse, 3.61:1
Final drive ratio 4.125:1
Reduction gears at axle 1200, 1.39:1; 1500, 1.26:1

SUSPENSION

One of the Transporter's most endearing and famous features, the Porsche-designed all-independent torsion bar system, is particularly respected for its ability to accept a lifetime of punishment and abuse, while at the same time giving the kind of ride quality and handling characteristics that put this vehicle light years ahead of its contemporaries.

With the ability to travel over a ploughed field, rough dusty track or smooth motorway at the same speed, the Transporter left its rivals well behind. For devotees of torsion bar springing, and there are millions worldwide, any other form of suspension is just not good enough. It is interesting that when

Volkswagen introduced the 1302S 1600 Beetle in 1970 with MacPherson strut front suspension, in order to give more luggage space, the Transporter soldiered on for another nine years with torsion bars.

Similar in layout to the system fitted to the Beetle and Porsche 356, the Transporter's suspension differs only in detail. At the front the suspension assembly comprises two tubular steel beams or axle tubes one above the other, and held rigidly in place by uprights welded on their outer ends. This is commonly referred to as the axle beam, and it is bolted to the chassis with six bolts, four of which pass through two further uprights close to the centre of the beam, and two at the centre of the beam. There are two grease nipples in each of the two tubes for lubricating the torsion bars, which Volkswagen recommended every 6000 miles.

The torsion bars are actually flat torsion leaves – five in the lower tube and four in the upper one – held together against twisting by a strong anchor block at the centre of each tube. In effect, this gives four torsion bars in all, with two in each side of the axle tubes. Independence of the suspension is afforded by two parallel trailing, or torsion, arms on the outer ends of the axle beam. These pivot on bearings located inside the torsion tubes and are attached on the outside with bolts.

At first the torsion arms were fitted with plastic bushes pressed into the axle tubes, but from March 1960 an outer needle roller bearing and an inner plastic and metal bush were used instead. During restoration, renewing these bearings, which are not needed too often, requires the use of special Volkswagen tools and professional expertise to avoid costly and time-consuming mistakes.

The outer ends of the trailing arms are attached to the steering knuckle and stub axles via adjustable link and king pins. These are fitted with three grease nipples which must be serviced every 1500 miles, or even 750-1000 miles on vehicles that are continually used on rough roads. Failure to do so will result in Ferrari-like bills to have the pins rebuilt.

The one-piece hubs and the brake drums ran on ball bearings until March 1960, taper roller bearings thereafter. An anti-roll bar was fitted from August 1960, and is attached to the lower of the two trailing arms with rubber-reinforced clips. Irrespective of mileage covered, the clips appear to have a reasonably long life of around 15 years, at which point they simply fall off with a 'ping' onto the road.

Except for the rear suspension of 'Barndoor' models, all Transporters were fitted with modern, non-adjustable, hydraulic telescopic shock absorbers, made by Boge until April 1963 and Fichtel & Sachs thereafter. At the rear of 'Barndoors' there were Boge or Hemscheidt lever-arm shock absorbers, which changed from single-acting to double-acting in August 1950. Front shock absorbers were bolted top and bottom to the uprights that form an integral part of the torsion bar tubes. Slightly inclined at an angle, the telescopic rear shock absorbers were bolted at the bottom to the base of the reduction gearbox casings, and at the top to a bracket welded to the chassis rail. Fitting new shock absorbers today is inevitably down to what is available, but Boge are the most common.

The rear suspension follows much the same principle as the front, with transverse torsion bars housed in cylindrical tubes on each side just in front of the rear wheels. Whereas the front torsion bars are divided into individual leaves, there are just two solid bars – one in each tube – at the rear. Initially, the bars were of 30mm (1.18in) diameter but were reduced to 29mm (1.14in) from March 1955, purely to soften the suspension a little. Even loyal German clientele, who traditionally enjoy firm suspension, found the early Transporters on the hard side of sensible, although this change was more to meet the needs of customers in North America. The torsion bars were altered again in August 1959, when they were reduced in length from 627mm (24.7in) to 553mm (21.8in) and in diameter to 22mm (0.87in).

The inner ends of the torsion bars are splined to fixed steel anchor blocks inside the centre of the torsion tubes, and the outer ends are splined to the trailing or radius arms – thin pieces of sheet steel that run longitudinally to and below the rear axles, where they are attached with four bolts to the inner casings of the hub gearboxes. Small spring plates are attached with bolts to the front of the trailing arms to close and seal the torsion bar tubes.

At the rear the suspension is really a cross between a trailing arm and pure swing axle system, in which cornering loads are taken up through the axle tube sockets on the side of the gearbox and final drive casing. The trailing arms are subjected to bending as the wheels move up and down in their arcs, although solid rubber bump stops keep a check on things getting out of hand on rough road surfaces.

With age and high mileage, the rear torsion bars have a tendency to lose some of their strength, a tell-tale sign being the degree of negative camber adopted by the wheels. Although negative camber improves roadholding and curbs the inherent tendency towards oversteer, it can lead to alarming tyre wear on the inside tread. The rear torsion bars can be adjusted to compensate for this inevitable tendency to sag, but in standard form the front suspension is not adjustable. If you cannot resist the urge to lower the ride height in the popular Cal-look style, never, even for a moment, be tempted to take the easy and inexpensive route of removing a torsion leaf or two. This is not sound engineering practice as it weakens the suspension and is potentially dangerous.

During the late 1950s and early 1960s Volkswagen made a number of small changes to the gearbox and rear axle – virtually all in the nature of 'widgets' – which lead me to wonder whether the company employed someone whose sole mission was both to baffle future Volkswagen historians and irritate mechanics in the dealer network. For restoration purposes today, however, the important changes involve the rear torsion bars. The inclination angle of the spring plate changed from 12° 30′ to 11° 30′ in January 1959, and the camber of the rear wheels was altered from 4° 30′ to 3° 30′. In August of the same year there were further changes with the spring plate inclination angle being altered to 16° 30′, but the camber angle remained the same. Setting up the rear suspension, so that the vehicle handles properly and does not develop a propensity for eating tyres, requires special tools and a fair degree of expertise. The removal of torsion bars, which are held in compression, should not be attempted by amateurs as they can cause serious injuries.

Hot Rod Special commented of the suspension in 1963: 'The truck and wagon suspension is basically the same as the sedan (Beetle) – all wheels are independent via transverse torsion bars and tubular shocks. As a consequence, the ride is good, far better than one would suppose from such a utilitarian vehicle. As long as the generous load limits are not surpassed, there is no need for any sort of overload springing. In fact, it would be difficult to figure out any means of adding it, except for heavier shocks or possibly an extra set all round.'

Just before production ended in 1967, *Motor's* road testers reckoned that the Microbus 'deals well with everything but waves on the road surface; a minor undulation taken at speed will cause the van to pitch markedly, but damping is effective. The pitching is most evident to the driver: those sitting amidships are less conscious of it.' This pitching is a characteristic of all Transporters and should not, after a lengthy rebuild, be taken as an indication that there is anything wrong with the suspension.

STEERING

With the driver sitting above the front wheels and the steering column ahead of the axle beam, the Transporter's steering is slightly more complex than the Beetle's, although there are obvious similarities between the two. Fitted with the ZF system, the steering box works on the worm-and-peg principle. The steering column fits directly into the gearbox and has an integral worm on its lower end. A peg carried by taper roller bearings and mounted on the steering arm is mated to the worm, the steering action being transmitted via a lever shaft to a drop arm.

In turn the drop arm is connected by a drag link to a swing lever, the latter being attached to a pair of steering knuckle arms via two tie rods. Unlike the Beetle, which has its steering box mounted on top of the torsion bar tube, the Transporter's unit is fitted to a bracket attached to the main chassis leg. This inevitably makes the steering gear vulnerable in front-end shunts, which is one reason why the main chassis

The hub reduction gearboxes – situated below the axle line – contain an upper and lower gear wheel enclosed in a cast iron case. Note that this vehicle is fitted with original pattern cross-ply tyres.

Patented in 1931, the Porsche-designed front suspension utilises transverse torsion bars, parallel trailing arms and hydraulic shock absorbers. The layout, seen on a 1953 'Barndoor', is similar to that of the Beetle and Porsche 356.

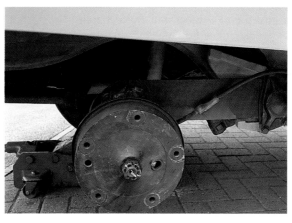

Transverse torsion bars and trailing arms were also used for the rear suspension, and lever-arm shock absorbers were fitted on 'Barndoor' models.

rails should be checked thoroughly for damage in the event of an accident.

The steering box is fully adjustable by turning a screw and locknut on the side of the casing, and the oil filler plug is situated on the top. Adjustments are not often necessary although wear in the steering gear may require them from time to time. The steering is fairly low-geared with 2.8 turns from lock to lock, and the turning circle between kerbs is 33ft (10.1m) on left lock and 35ft (10.7m) on right lock.

A steering damper was fitted from March 1955, coinciding with the lovely three-spoke steering wheel being changed for the more modern but less attractive two-spoker. Stabilus or Hemscheidt originally supplied steering dampers, but Boge units were in general use after 1960. A 2mm thick shim between the hexagonal screw and the steering damper eye was fitted from February 1956, and the tie rods on right-hand drive vehicles were altered from January 1959, the left-hand one shortened from 814mm (32.1in) to 807mm (31.8in) and the right-hand one lengthened from 318mm (12.5in) to 325mm (12.8in). The wall thickness of the steering column tube was increased from 1.5mm to 2mm in October 1963.

Many left-hand drive Transporters – exactly how many is not known – were fitted with ATE steering boxes. Apart from being stamped ATE on the casing, they have a number of components – steering box cover, guide tube, adjusting screw, lockplate and bearing flange for the steering column tube – which are not interchangeable with the ZF steering box.

Both types of steering box hold half a pint of SAE 90 Hypoid oil. The level should be checked every 3000 miles, and topped up if necessary to the lower edge of the filler plug hole.

With such a relatively large diameter steering wheel, the Transporter should always feel light, and by the standards of the day it is also directionally precise. Oddly, there does not appear to be much difference in feel with and without a steering damper.

BRAKING

Unlike the Beetle, all Transporters were fitted with hydraulically-operated drum brakes from the start of production. The front brakes have two leading shoes and the rears are fitted with one leading and one trailing shoe. The handbrake is mechanically operated on the rear wheels by two cables which run partially in conduits. The front drums were originally fitted with one main cylinder, and each drum has a serrated adjuster. Twin cylinders were fitted from March 1955, but single-cylinder operation was retained at the rear.

The rears also have serrated nuts, which are adjusted by inserting a screwdriver in the back plates. The brake pedal is connected to the master cylinder by a short pushrod, and the fluid reservoir is situated under an inspection plate in the cab floor. Volkswagen recommended its own brake fluid, or Lockheed, but warned strongly against the use of other brands.

Changes to the braking system up to March 1955 were minor. From August 1950 the front brake cylinders were reduced in diameter from 22.2mm (0.87in) to 19.5mm (0.77in), and from March 1952 the fluid reservoir no longer had a float. Reinforced front hubs were fitted from March 1953, and the wheel cylinders were mounted with two bolts instead of four from May 1954.

From March 1955, at the same time as twin cylinders were fitted to the front drums, the front brake shoes were increased in width from 40mm (1.57in) to 50mm (1.97in), while those at the rear remained unchanged at 40mm (1.57in). As a result of this modification at the front, the braking surface area increased from 700sq cm (108.5sq in) to 836sq cm (129.6sq in). At the same time the master cylinder was increased in diameter from 19.05mm (0.75in) to 22.2mm (0.87in), and both front and rear wheel cylinders were enlarged, the former from 20.2mm (0.79in) to 35.5mm (1.00in), the latter from 19.05mm (0.75in) to 22.2mm (0.87in).

All Split-screen Transporters used single-circuit brakes with a relatively small master cylinder, although from 1963 the front and rear circuits were made independent from each other by the expedient of a tandem master cylinder.

There were fairly fundamental braking differences between 1200 and 1500 engined vehicles. The 1200s had 230mm (9.06in) diameter drums, whereas the more powerful vehicle's drums were slightly larger at 247mm (9.72in). The linings on the 1500s were also wider at 55mm (2.17in) for the front and 45mm (1.78in) for the rear.

Contemporary magazines rarely praised the Transporter's ability to stop, although owners generally enthused about the brakes. The truth is that they were adequate, but far from startling and not entirely immune to fade, especially in hilly country when the heat build-up could never dissipate quickly enough to give full confidence. Those who got on well with the brakes, and many did, only realised how comparatively poor they were after driving the later Bay-window models fitted with front disc brakes.

CONCLUSION

That the original Split-screen Transporter lasted so long in production – 17 years was remarkable even by contemporary German standards – surprised Volkswagen as much as its customers. But it proved to be a dependable workhorse that could be used and abused for many years without giving major trouble.

Even by the beginning of the 1960s, however, motoring was beginning to change. Many customers actually encouraged Volkswagen not to change the Transporter – most loved it in its original form that much – but in certain quarters safety was becoming a publicly debated issue. In America the consumer group led by Ralph Nader began to criticise motor manufacturers for the way in which they constructed vehicles. And the impact this group made – for good or bad – led to Nader's ideas being enshrined in legislation before the decade was out.

Along with all the world's other manufacturers, Volkswagen was forced to put aside many established values and adapt to new ones. The classic Splittie bowed out from Wolfsburg in 1967, although the vehicle continued to be built in Brazil until 1976. Enthusiasts the world over mourned its passing – and they still do! However, Volkswagen was not about to let its loyal customers down. In August 1967, the company launched the Split-screen's successor, another classic – albeit a very different animal from the vehicle it replaced – which in time would become as highly regarded as the original 'box on wheels'.

BAY-WINDOWS (1967-79)

After the production of 1.8 million Split-screen Transporters, a wholly new model was launched in August 1967. Now popularly referred to as the 'Bay-window' Transporter, it differed from its predecessor in nearly all respects. Volkswagen's philosophy of providing a 'box on wheels' had not changed, of course, and the engine was still air-cooled and positioned at the rear, but there was a most welcome increase in performance, the roadholding was improved and, as the body was lengthened by 100mm (4in), there was more interior space.

The styling was different but the new vehicle was still instantly recognisable as a Volkswagen. By this stage the Transporter was not so much a vehicle, but a way of life. Even in Microbus de luxe guise, the Volkswagen had never been a glamorous vehicle, and was never intended as such, but it had always had an image that for most people conjured up the spirit of the 1960s. Little has changed…

Arguably not as pretty as the Splittie, the Bay-window certainly made an impression and sales continued to increase. Despite the considerable efforts of other manufacturers to improve upon the basic design of the 'box' with their own products, its versatility remained unmatched. Ralph Nader and company had never been fans of swing-axle rear suspension, or many of the other features of air-cooled Volkswagens, but their efforts actually did Volkswagen a big favour in the long term. With each improvement came more customers. By the end of Bay-window production in 1979, 4.8 million Transporters had been built all told – quite remarkable.

It is difficult to appreciate the quantity of work performed by the designers and production engineers during the planning stage of the new model because, unlike the Split-screen Transporter line-up, the Bay-window range was comprehensive and complete right from the beginning of production. The new range included a Panelvan and High-roof version, Microbus, Kombi, Pick-ups in Double-cab, Single-cab and extended platform forms, and the top-of-the-range Microbus de luxe. The latter was dubbed the Clipper for the first two years of production but was known simply as the 'L' version thereafter.

The launch of the Bay-window coincided with the public debut of a completely revised Beetle and naturally the two vehicles shared several components, such as the headlamps. Today, *aficionados* continue to debate whether the revisions to both vehicles were done at the expense of a loss of character, but for those who needed a good, dependable utility vehicle this argument is largely irrelevant – it was from the driving seat that the majority delivered an opinion. And their opinion was overwhelmingly that the Bay-window was a superior animal.

There was a greater feeling of space, improved forward visibility through the large, panoramic, one-piece windscreen, a higher top speed of 65mph, better acceleration for safer overtaking, more comfortable upholstery and a generally more modern feel. Despite the passage of nearly 20 years, and two further replacement models from Volkswagen during this time, the styling of the Bay-window – and thousands are still in use around the world – does not appear to have dated.

In March 1968 the American magazine *Popular Imported Cars* concluded: 'All in all, the VW 'boxes' have been considerably improved in all the important areas. We leave it to you to decide if beautiful is the word to describe them, but they have got to be driven to be believed.'

Interestingly, there was very little press criticism of the new vehicle throughout its entire production period, although some features perhaps warranted it. The suspension, for example, was considerably softer than that of its predecessor. Although this generally found favour in the North American market, few owners in Africa, Australia and mainland Europe ever got used to the wallowing and pitching that characterised the handling on rough roads.

By the end of the 1960s the Bay-window had as large a cult following as the Splittie, particularly in the USA where, like the Beetle, the Transporter's completely classless image endeared it to ordinary folk and the rich and famous alike. As *Road Test* magazine noted in 1971: 'One of the latest automotive fads, particularly in trend-setting California, is the use of a delivery van for personal transportation. You see all manner and types of vans with curtained windows, rear shackles lengthened to hoist the rear end, fat rear tires, surfboards mounted on top or protruding from the rear door, and eight-track stereo blaring away. It makes a lot of sense. You can carry a staggering volume of people and/or sports equipment in a van: people have been known to live in them and by adding a few seats, the utility of a station wagon is obtained at a lot less cost.'

The writer of this test neatly sums up Transporter ownership at the time – and little has changed since. Droves of owners, virtually all of them Volkswagen enthusiasts, can still be seen using their mounts for a variety of purposes, particularly in the summer months. And when components fail or bodywork rusts away, they carry out the necessary repairs and take to the wheel once again. It is true: old Transporters never die.

BODYWORK & CHASSIS

Because Volkswagen's draughtsmen started with a fresh sheet of paper in designing the Bay-window model, no body panels are interchangeable with the Split-screen vehicles. And although the two models are as different as chalk and cheese in many respects, the same design process and philosophy was applied to both. Unitary construction was retained, of course, with the sturdy chassis frame being integrated into the main structure of the body.

Nicknamed the Bay-window after its large, one-piece windscreen, the second-generation Transporter was launched in August 1967. Although it was endowed with less character than the Splittie, production rose inexorably upwards.

This all-original Dutch-registered Clipper L, chassis number 240 200 8166 built on 18 August 1969, is owned by Charles Dams, who bought it from its original owner. Compared with the Split-screen Microbus de luxe's four passenger compartment side windows, Bay-window design was simplified to just two large windows. Note configuration of opening quarterlights on these windows: in the sliding door on one side, in the rearmost window on the other.

Owned from new by Jerry Spellman and with 171,000 miles on the clock, this concours Microbus is chassis number 220 212 8941 built in February 1970. Pretty and purposeful, but de luxe type additional chrome (for VW badge, fresh air grille, window frames and waistline strip) and US-spec overriders arguably overburden the simple aesthetics. Middle window on driver's side could have optional opening quarterlight, but not rearward window on the other side – the sliding door would have mangled it.

At the front the partially double-skinned and curved nose panel – now without the famous Y-shaped swage lines of its predecessor – had apertures for the headlamps in much the same position as before, but a new feature was the rectangular grille below the windscreen for the revised cabin ventilation system. Cut-outs for the indicators were below the headlamps at first, but above them from August 1972. Welded to the front (or nose) panel are the windscreen pillars, which are joined in turn at their bases to the lower A posts, sturdy pieces that run down and are welded to the outer wings or wheelarch panels. At the base of the front panel is a separate valance or closing panel.

A single panel is used for the cab floor and, like so many other pieces, it is corrugated for added strength. The B pillar runs from the roof to the front of the outer and inner sill, or rocker panel, finishing just behind the rear of the front wheel arches. Welded to the inside of the B pillars are the sheet steel frames for the driver's and passenger's seat backrests. The seat bases are in two pieces, the outer ones being welded to the inside of the wheelarch panels, which in effect form the inner wings, and the inner ones – generally known as the seat boxes – being welded to the two main chassis longitudinal members.

The floor of the cargo-cum-passenger area is in two pieces and corrugated. At the sides of the vehicle, these panels are welded to the sills and at the front to the lower part of the cab seat structures. At the rear of the floor is a large panel which is stepped to clear the gearbox and rear suspension assembly that rises steeply, and this is joined to a horizontal panel that forms the rear luggage space above the engine.

The rear side panels are divided into two large pieces on each side, the lower one including the wheelarches, the upper containing a cut-out for windows on Kombis and Microbuses. The lower panel on the right-hand side of the body also includes the fuel filler neck, which was repositioned further back on the body from August 1971 to make it accessible with the sliding door open. A further change to

Both Single-cab and Double-cab Pick-ups were available from the beginning, and the relatively few survivors do not come much better than Steve Daniel's pristine US-spec Single-cab, chassis number 268 026 037 dating from September 1967. Chromed bumpers are a personal modification as they were optionally available only on the Microbus de luxe after the new bumper style arrived in August 1972 – but they look great on this workhorse.

Pick-up is essentially a 'cut-down' Panelvan with a locker bed and drop-down sides; locker bed was even larger than the Split-screen version, and optionally could be accessed from both sides. Note how tail-flap has tiny apertures to allow tail lamps to shine through; this feature was unique to US-spec Pick-ups and Double-cabs sold to the German Army, the latter seen (below) in enlarged – and glazed – form to suit post-August 1971 lamp clusters.

this configuration occurred in August 1972 when the fuel filler flap was deleted, requiring the panel to be modified to suit the exposed filler cap. All body glass was supplied by Sekurit, the windscreen being laminated, and the people-carrying vehicles have just two large rectangular windows per side.

To the rear of the upper side panels are the louvred air intakes for the engine's cooling system, instead of being cut into the lower side panels where they were on the Split-screen models. These were enlarged and made squarer when the 1700 engine was fitted for the 1972 model year. At the rear the tailgate is hinged at the top, has a large cut-out for the window glass and a small aperture at the bottom for the centrally positioned lock. The tailgate actually pivots on two hinges on a narrow transverse panel welded into the roof panel and the top quarter panels.

Below what is roughly the waist line of the vehicle are large rear quarters which include cut-outs for the tail lamps. The engine lid sits between these two rear quarters and is attached with two top-mounted

external hinges, which are fitted to a very narrow panel below the tailgate. This lid was also enlarged for the 1972 model year to improve access to the 1700 engine. A valance sits immediately below the engine lid and, like the one fitted to the Split-screen, was detachable until August 1971, then welded into place.

The roof, made in a single piece, is the largest body panel. On luxury Microbuses this panel has an aperture for the steel sliding sunroof, an extra-cost option on the other models.

The chassis, or floor frame, which is welded directly to the underside of the bodywork, is to a simple design and would not look too out of place on a vintage Bentley. It comprises two box-section longitudinal members, which run the length of the vehicle. A curved cross support sits immediately behind the valance panel, and there is a main front crossmember just in front of the axle assembly.

Behind this the base for the cab seats is formed by the seat boxes and side member inserts, which are positioned roughly vertically on top of the longitudinals. At this point the longitudinals curve upwards to clear the front suspension assembly. The front outriggers, which support the outer extremities of the bodywork, sit below the lower B pillars and the middle ones are positioned below the lower C posts. The middle outriggers sit on the outside of the main rear crossmember, in the same way that the front outriggers are positioned on the outside of the front crossmember. Two further outriggers sit a short way behind these, below the C posts.

Close to the rear of the frame and directly behind the rear outriggers is the transverse tube that houses the rear torsion bars. Unlike the Beetle's suspension, the Transporter's torsion bar tubes form an integral part of the chassis frame and, for added strength, there

Like its Single-cab sister, Double-cab Pick-up came with the option of a tarpaulin. This vehicle, chassis number 266 211 8516, is owned by Andrew Gdula and dates from February 1976. Note optional head restraints for front seats, and flag-holder on B-pillar that indicates German Army origins.

A mobile barn! With doors and lids open, it is easier to appreciate just how much space there is inside a Bus.

are additional metal supports welded between the two tubes and the main longitudinal members. In the centre of the frame between the two longitudinals is a long cylindrical tube running through the rear and centre crossmembers and up through the cab floor, and acting as a heater conduit from the exhaust heat exchangers through to the cabin.

The Single-cab and Double-cab Pick-ups are very similar in construction except that the cab roof panel is smaller, of course, and never carried the option of a sunroof. Both vehicles have corrugated flat beds with drop side panels and tailgate. As before, the side panels and tailgate were single panelled with a reinforcing framework, the former being attached with three hinges, the latter with two. Because the side flaps on the Double-cab are shorter, they have just two hinges on each side. Both types of Pick-up have the engine cooling louvres in the side panels above the rear

wheel arches in three vertical banks of three – an important difference between the trucks and other models. The extended platform Pick-ups have a West-falia-made wooden bed, side flaps and tailgate.

All second-generation Transporters, with the obvious exception of the trucks, have a sliding door rather than the old-fashioned 'pull-out' one fitted to the Split-screens. The sliding door was positioned, as before, on the opposite side to the driver, although a second one could be ordered for the driver's side as an extra-cost option. Single-cab and Double-cab Pick-ups have a locker bed, access to which is through a top-hinged door on the opposite side to the driver. This door has two hinges and a small aperture for the lock. An additional locker bed door on the driver's side was an extra-cost option.

The cab doors are similar in construction to those of the Split-screen, with a single skin clinched over

US-spec Microbus automatic, chassis number 224 213 5434 built in April 1974 and owned by Jim Mattison, who still keeps this 87,000-mile vehicle in daily use ferrying his family of five children around home in Rhode Island, USA. Many detail changes were made to the exterior in August 1971, '72 and '73: note bumper style, front indicators, position and size of VW emblem, protruding rear lamp 'plinths', style of passenger compartment door handle, fuel filler and engine air vent.

By the mid-1970s Volkswagen admitted that it had run out of ideas for improving the Transporter, and this Panelvan (chassis number 218 209 0620) from April 1978 looks no different from one made four years earlier. Richard Searles bought this one new and always intended to keep it beyond retirement, protecting it carefully through all the years it served as his everyday workhorse. Nowadays he runs a similarly cherished modern Type 4 van for work as a builder.

the top of an inner framework, but they are larger and the window frames are an integral part rather than being detachable as before. Double-cabs have just one door, again on the opposite side to the driver, for access to the rear cab compartment; the opposite side has a large panel with a square aperture for a window in the upper side panel, and a lower panel behind the driver's door.

The fuel tank is located in front of the engine below the horizontal panel that forms the rear luggage area, except on Pick-up trucks where the tank is positioned behind two detachable panels at the rear of the locker bed. These panels are detachable simply to facilitate removal of the fuel tank.

As before, the High-roof delivery van could be fitted with a taller-than-standard sliding side door. Like its Split-screen counterpart, this vehicle was primarily aimed at the clothing trade, and the tall door was a huge advantage in improving access to the load area. The High-roof delivery van's load capacity

is 6.2cu m (219cu ft), a substantial gain over the standard Panelvan's 5.0cu m (177cu ft).

Interestingly, in an attempt to save weight the High-roof's roof panel was made of glass-fibre in one piece and bonded to the top of the bodywork. This was an unusual material for Volkswagen to consider because, like the majority of mainstream motor manufacturers, the company was fairly sceptical about its durability and longevity. Daimler-Benz constructed just one 300SL 'Gullwing' coupé of glass-fibre in 1955, and shelved the idea immediately afterwards. The then-new material had a 'kit-car' image, but the passage of time has proved Volkswagen and a good many others – such as Lotus, Chevrolet and Ferrari – absolutely right in using this non-rusting material for body panels.

From the beginning of production, the entire underside of the chassis was protected with a thick coat of underseal which, apart from doing its intended job reasonably well, also had the effect of reducing

A remarkable vehicle by any standards. Craufurd Matthews' June 1978 Kombi, chassis number 238 214 7355, regularly wins concours awards despite being used daily and still spending its entire life outdoors. It is yet another one-owner-from-new vehicle, originally bought in Brussels but later imported to the UK (hence its Y registration of 1982/83).

Unlike Microbuses, the Kombi – the 'no-frills' people carrier – only came in single colours. The breed lacks a 'waistline' trim strip, passenger compartment quarterlights and bright trim around fixed windows, but this one has optional rubber bumper inserts and chromed VW emblem.

mechanical and road noise inside the cabin. Volkswagen went a step further and insulated the cab floor with a felt material and fitted rubber panels under the wheelarches.

By the end of the 1960s, passenger safety had become uppermost in the minds of world legislatures, particularly in North America. For the 1970 model year, the Transporter's doors were fitted with stronger inner frames to provide better protection in side impacts. At the same time the body was made more rigid by stiffening the four main body hoops that rise from the floor and reinforce the main roof panel. Continuing on the safety theme, the cab floor was redesigned in August 1972 to include a 'crumple' zone that would deform progressively in the event of a head-on collision. The pressing behind the handle on the sliding door was modified at the same time, to suit the revised handle.

After the oil crisis of 1973, Volkswagen, along with most manufacturers, dropped down a gear and

concentrated its efforts on making its engines more efficient, which is why there were very few further modifications of a non-mechanical nature – Transporters from 1973, 1974 and 1975 are outwardly almost indistinguishable.

By 1976 Volkswagen admitted that development of the second-generation Transporter was over. The official brochure for this model year, which was as typically unflamboyant as the vehicles it featured, made it perfectly clear that there was no point in making further changes for the sake of it. It comments: 'The VW Commercial has nothing new to offer. Which is precisely what makes it so remarkable. The way it stands, it has been tested, selected, driven and found acceptable over 4 million times to date.

'Sure, in all the years it's been around, it was worked on and improved, again and again. But it was the same basic idea which was behind its success in the past 26 years. Which shows that we were right in sticking to it.'

The VW roundel was white plastic (left) on most models, but chromed (right) on Microbus L. From August 1972 the roundel was smaller (bottom left) and placed lower on the nose panel.

It was hardly necessary for identification, but Volkswagen name was always fitted to rear – normally to left on tailgate but centrally on Pick-up models – until August 1972. Thereafter only versions with newly-available automatic transmission had a badge, in a different style.

Front indicators were placed below the headlamps until August 1972, then moved above them (and made squarer and larger) to make them more clearly visible to oncoming traffic.

Tail lamps were initially the same as those used on late Splitties, with indicator segment in amber for most markets but red for the US; when optional reversing lamps were fitted they were placed above these units. New tail lamps from August 1971 were larger and included integral reversing lamps.

BODY TRIM

Volkswagen did not exactly go over the top in adorning the bodies of the Bay-window models. But what was attached was both in keeping with contemporary trends and the utilitarian nature of the vehicle. As customers had come to expect, though, the external features, down to the VW roundels, were of exceptionally high quality.

The Hella headlamps are the same as those fitted to post-August 1967 Beetles, but lack a plastic insert between the chrome bezel and the bodywork. Two beam adjusters are incorporated into the bezel, and a single Philips screw secures the unit to the bodywork. To begin with the indicators, also made by Hella, were placed below the headlamps towards the outside of the front panel. Rectangular in shape and with a chromed trim around their perimeter, these had amber lenses on European and American vehicles.

A large V-over-W motif in white plastic was placed

in the centre of the nose panel between the head-lamps on all models except the Luxury Microbus, which had a chromed item. In recent times many owners have taken to painting these items in various colours, to the point where originals are not a particularly common sight nowadays. These roundels have also been a target for thieves.

The wrap-around bumpers are much larger, heavier and supposedly stronger than the Split-screen versions. They were altered in response to American legislation, which is a pity because they are so conspicuous that, at the front, they threatened to turn the happy, smiling face into something altogether more purposeful for an age that was beginning to feel the pain of city traffic congestion. The bumpers were painted white, although Luxury Microbuses could be fitted with chromed ones as an extra-cost option after the bumper revisions of August 1972. The ends of the earlier type of front bumper are flattened and covered with rubber to form a cab step.

Bumper overriders with rubber inserts were also extra-cost options, but few owners outside North America, where they were almost a necessity by the early 1970s, bothered to order them. In some markets rubber inserts for the bumpers were also offered as extra-cost options. Where they appeared, the inserts were in two pieces, divided by the registration number plate. British brochures listed these inserts with anodised trim as standard on Luxury Microbuses, but it is clearly not the case that they were fitted to all vehicles.

Also on the front panel on the Luxury versions of the Microbus is a piece of alloy trim placed around the perimeter of the air intake louvres, but this did little to enhance the appearance of these vehicles and was dropped for August 1972. By the end of the 1960s, other manufacturers were beginning to use matt black body trim, but not Volkswagen, whose many customers still considered bits of chrome and alloy to be something of a luxury.

Incidentally, many Bay-window models can be seen sporting the spare wheel, usually covered in a vinyl glove, attached vertically to the front panel. This is a useful way of creating more space inside the vehicle, but this modification was usually carried out by Camper specialists or by owners privately.

Due to the shape of the Transporter, there is no naturally convenient position on the bodywork for a radio aerial; the flatness of almost every panel ensured that an aerial would stick out like a sore thumb. But where a radio was fitted, the aerial was usually placed on one side of the front panel, often on the outside curved part between the headlamps and windscreen. Some dealers and owners fitted the aerial in the centre of the roof above the windscreen.

Supplied by Bosch, the long windscreen wipers were the first to be fitted by Volkswagen that actually gave reasonably good sweep on the windscreen, the short, quaint items of yesteryear mercifully gone for

US-spec vehicles had circular reflectors (amber at front, red at rear) on the flanks until August 1969, but then rectangular reflectors (with same colour difference) were introduced to meet new legislation.

good. As with the majority of vehicles from this era, they worked parallel to each other, were positioned below the windscreen on the outside of the front panel, and were seated to the bodywork by rubber grommets. A single washer nozzle, also with a rubber grommet, was positioned to the right of each wiper shaft. The wiper arms have a matt grey finish and, in the absence of mindless vandalism, appear to be virtually indestructible.

On the Luxury Microbus the window rubbers, including the windscreen, were trimmed with slim

Mounted high on rear quarters, engine cooling vents were unobtrusive to begin with and perfectly adequate for 1600 engine, but they had to be enlarged in August 1971 to suit 1700 engine. Pick-ups had to have a different arrangement, so louvre pattern found on late Splitties was continued; note red side reflector on this 1967 US version.

alloy mouldings. Bend these at your peril during restoration work – they will never again fit properly if you do.

Luxury Microbuses have alloy mouldings along the flanks. Whereas contemporary Beetles have just a thin moulding strip along their sides, the Transporter's size led to the fitting of a wider strip. The moulding is in separate pieces, with one for the cab door, a tiny piece for the B pillar, another that stretches across the middle section or sliding door, and another across the rear side panel. An additional strip wraps around the

curved rear quarters and extends across the rear panel below the back window. From August 1974 the design of these strips changed to include a rubber insert, their position changed from on the raised waistline section to just below it, and the matching strip across the tail was deleted. Because of the way in which attitudes to brightwork have changed, many Volkswagen enthusiasts agree that the unadorned Kombis and cargo carriers are aesthetically better balanced than Luxury Microbuses.

American-spec Transporters differ in that they have side markers. Initially these took the form of circular amber reflectors positioned on the cab doors close to the front bumper, and a further pair with red lenses on the rear lower quarters behind the wheelarches. These were changed in August 1969 for rectangular reflectors, which were usefully larger from a road safety point of view but did little to enhance the vehicle's aesthetics.

Mirrors were fitted as standard on both sides of the vehicle across the range, and are bolted directly to the cab doors below and slightly in front of the rear frame of the quarterlight. They are rectangular in shape and on passenger-carrying vehicles they have aluminium alloy backs, which left the factory with a satin finish; 'commercials' had grey painted mirror backs as standard. These are attached to the doors by upward-pointing arms of chromed steel, are manually adjustable, and are designed to fold backwards or forwards on impact. Along with the windscreen wipers, the mirrors appear to last forever, which is just as well because originals are now difficult to obtain.

In keeping with the vehicle's purpose and image, the rear end was kept fairly simple. The tail lamps were initally the same as those fitted to late Split-screens: they are rectangular in shape with the corners rounded off, and have 'silvered' frames and rubber inserts for seating to the bodywork. The one-piece lenses have an amber sector at the top for the indicator, a red reflector in the centre, and a stop and tail lamp at the bottom. As with later Splitties, US models had slightly different tail lamps with a red indicator segment and a separate chromed bezel. Twin reversing lights with white lenses were offered as an extra-cost option in all markets, but few early vehicles were fitted with them.

Both the tailgate and engine lid have a small opening handle with an integral circular push-button and locks. These handles are more in the mould of finger latches, and are seated to the panels with black plastic inserts. Both the latches and locks were chromed to the very highest standards and, even on very old Transporters, often retain a deep shine.

The tailgate also features a small Volkswagen name plate on the lower left-hand side, or in the centre above the engine lid on Pick-ups. This badge is made of alloy with a bright finish, and the letters are in capitals. Curiously, the badge did not appear for the 1973 model year. At this time Transporters were selling so well that most people were familiar with the sight of them, so Volkswagen presumably surmised that there was little need to further identify the vehicle by adding a badge. A small badge costs comparatively little to make but adds up to a lot of money when produced in Volkswagen volumes, so it is probably correct to conclude that this was a penny-pinching exercise, and a mean one too.

The external cab door handles, immensely strong with an integral lock and a superb chromed finish, are similar to those fitted to contemporary Beetles. As with the Beetle, the design changed in August 1968 when the push-button was replaced by a trigger release on the underside of the handle. The handle fitted to the sliding side door initially had an integral lock and turned upwards roughly through 90 degrees for closing, but after August 1972 the lock was fitted into the door panel below a redesigned handle that turned upwards less far. The lockable lid for the under-bed compartment on Pick-ups is operated by a neat, chromed push-button.

Double-cab Pick-ups normally have a rubber bump-stop on the cab door to prevent the rear side cab door being damaged when opened, but this useful addition was not fitted in all markets. Pick-ups also had pairs of these small bump stops on the bed's side flaps and tailgate.

As before, the Pick-ups could be fitted with bows and a canvas tarpaulin, but this was always an extra-

After the first year of production, new design of cab door handle in August 1968 remained a 'fixed' type, with trigger release instead of push-button.

Release handle for sliding side door changed in August 1972, with panel recess altered to suit. First type has integral lock and moves 90 degrees upwards for closing (note original wording on this Dutch-registered Microbus); second type has separate lock and moves upwards less far (original '8 people' label on this Belgian-sourced Kombi was an insurance requirement in that market).

Both engine lid and tailgate for the most part had a push-button release (with convenient finger latch) finished in high-quality chrome, but Volkswagen economy measures in latter years included fitting cheaper plastic handles from August 1975.

During the first four years of production the sliding door inconveniently overlapped the fuel filler flap, which concealed a filler cap with VW motif. Solution was to move filler rearwards in August 1971 – and also to cheapen the appearance by deleting the flap in August 1972.

Bumper design changed in August 1972. Early type is bumper of rounded profile and wrap-round design with integral cab step, while later energy-absorbing type has different shape and step is inside the cab. Both types could be had with rubber inserts along the blades, and also with overriders for the US.

cost option. Despite its practical value, the canvas was never especially popular, as the majority of owners, particularly those in the building trade, preferred to expose their tools and tackle to the weather rather than shell out good money for a protective covering. Original items are comparatively rare, and those that do exist are usually past their best.

Changes to external body features were few and far between. In August 1971 the tail lamp cluster was re-shaped and made much bigger. Instead of the neat, rounded-off rectangular units, there were long vertical clusters with integral reversing lights at the base. From August 1972 the front indicators were moved from below the headlamps to a position high on the panel, apparently to make them more easily seen by other road users. As they were housed on the outsides of the fresh-air grille, they changed the frontal appearance of the vehicle, arguably for the better too. Their amber lenses were square and, to some, they resemble eyebrows above the headlamps. Curiously, clear lenses, which were used on many American-spec vehicles from other manufacturers, were not fitted to US-bound Transporters. At the same time the VW roundel was made smaller, perhaps as a result of another of Volkswagen's penny-pinching exercises, and placed lower on the nose panel.

Also from August 1972, all Transporters were fitted with slightly larger, energy-absorbing bumpers. The cab step, which was previously part of the front bumper, was sited inside the cab door across the range

Grey windscreen wipers (below) made by Bosch and designed to park on right; accompanying washer nozzles are seated with plastic inserts. Among the host of detail body changes in August 1972, the engine lid became slightly shallower (right) and even the panel bulge housing the number plate light was altered. Generous recess for the plate itself catered for all shapes and sizes; the smaller hinges show

this late engine lid to be a post-August 1975 version. Quarterlight windows (bottom) were fixed and black-framed as standard, but opening versions with chromed trim were usually fitted to people-carrying vehicles. 'Theft-proof' catch opens in two stages, but plastic knob is prone to snapping off. Throughout production all models had this mirror style on both sides.

in all markets. As a result, the bumper was no longer of wrap-around style. For Microbuses these revised bumpers also had a full-width rubber insert across the leading edge as standard (an extra-cost option on other models).

An extra-cost option introduced across the range in August 1973 was headlamp washer jets built into the bumper overriders. This was a clever piece of marketing, because if you wanted this little tweak you had to pay extra for overriders too. For the remaining years of production, nothing more changed externally other than the adoption in August 1975 of black plastic instead of chromed metal for the locks on the engine lid and tailgate. There is, after all, only so much that can be done to improve body trim, fittings and interior equipment.

Two-tone paint schemes were standard on Luxury versions of the Microbus, except where Pastel White was specified. In fact, throughout the 1970s Volkswagen offered several whacky paint colours which date the Bay-windows considerably more than the overall design of the vehicle. In this respect, though, they are no different from contemporary Porsche 911s painted in Roman Purple or BMW 2002s in a memorable bright green.

Down the years Transporters have been fitted with all sorts of accessories, including alloy finger plates behind the door handles, alloy mouldings to protect the wheelarches against stone chippings, chin spoilers and a host of other 'go-faster goodies', most of which trap moisture and cause corrosion.

Designed more with safety and comfort in mind, Bay-window cab interior – this one from 1969 Clipper L – makes greater use of soft plastic, seats are bigger and more comfortable, and instrumentation is more comprehensive. Although lacking Split-screen's character, the Bay is much more user-friendly. Note air duct along door trim and the tubes it links with either side of door opening, in order to heat passenger compartment. Winding windows and recessed door handles were common to all models, but two-tone panelling and padded armrests were reserved for luxury Microbuses.

INTERIOR

There was little disagreement upon the Bay-window's launch that its interior appointments and space utilisation in all models were just about peerless. By today's standards, even the best equipped Microbus appears to be comparatively stark but, in typical German fashion, it was entirely functional. And these vehicles were purchased in droves for this reason.

A much bigger vehicle than the Split-screen, the new version had improved all-round vision thanks to larger windows. The interior was light, bright and airy, and so modern in layout that Bay-windows have never really dated except in detail – just one of the many reasons why thousands are still being used as everyday transport.

Naturally, trim levels and interior equipment varied from one model to the next, and the Pick-up and Panelvan, of course, were the most austere. By

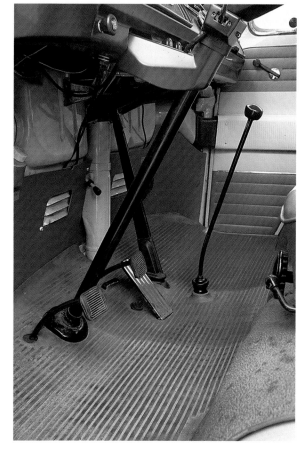

1967, however, Volkswagen was exporting its products to 140 countries world-wide, and vehicle specifications often varied between markets. Thankfully for restorers today the overall picture is one of uniformity, although the list of extra-cost options became increasingly long as the years went by.

In all models the seats are to Volkswagen's traditional form of construction with a simple metal framework, low-profile spring core cushions, and firm padding. Both the squabs and backrests are much bigger, more comfortable and body-hugging than the Split-screen's. Volkswagen claimed in its official advertising literature that the backrests are 'shoulder high', which they clearly are not. The seat covers are made of hard-wearing vinyl, which is piped around the outsides and, as before, has the advantage of being easy to clean.

In the cab the seats are fluted longitudinally and have a ridged pattern, whereas passenger seats in the rear are fluted transversely but retain the same ridged finish. The Luxury version of the Microbus has two-tone 'air permeable' covers to allow the seats to 'breathe' more easily, which was perceived to be of benefit in hot weather.

In standard form all models except the Pick-up came with two separate seats in the cab – the driver's seat being adjustable fore and aft to nine different positions, the backrest adjustable to any position – with a walkway between them to allow access to the

Padded for safety and finished in black to prevent windscreen reflections, the Bay's plastic dashboard was in keeping with contemporary design. Instruments comprise fuel gauge, speedometer and clock as standard on Clipper L, but radio was an extra-cost option on all models; note gearchange transfer on ashtray. Gear lever is longer than Split-screen's (and feels sloppy and vague), pedals rise almost vertically from floor, brake fluid reservoir is sited behind front panel.

Luxury, Volkswagen style. Two-tone Clipper L seats are in vinyl, and matching side panels have bright mouldings and substantial armrests; near-side third seat with folding backrest was standard, although a two-seater bench was optional – but with no reduction in price!

In luggage compartment, L version came with rigid plastic cover for spare wheel, carpeted floor, chromed restraining bar on rear seat, and a pair of diagonal bars to protect adjacent windows.

compartment or a full dividing wall with a built-in rectangular window. High-roof Panelvans had a walkway between the two vertical panels dividing the load area from the cab.

Anchorage points for seat belts were standard but the belts themselves were an extra-cost option, although most vehicles appear to have had them fitted by dealers. In the cab they were of the dismal 'hang-loose' breed, but most owners have switched to modern inertia reels. Seat belts for rear seat passengers were also extra-cost options, but these are two-point lap belts like the one fitted to the inner bench seat in the cab. From a safety point of view, these should be 'binned' at the earliest opportunity – they are potentially very dangerous.

An easy-to-clean vinyl headlining, coloured Cloud White, was fitted to the cab roof across the range and in the rear compartment of passenger-carrying versions. The headlining does not extend as far as the A-pillars, as this area is finished in body colour. The interior cab door panels are made of a fibreboard material covered in hard-wearing vinyl and fastened with clips pressed into small rubber grommets. In freight-carrying Transporters, the interior panels are plain except for the flutes at the top of each and a 'swage' line roughly across the middle.

The cab door handles are similar to Beetle items and take the form of small, chromed finger latches recessed into the panel for safety reasons. On Panel-

rear passenger compartment. As Volkswagen made clear, this was a great advantage in controlling unruly children without mother or father having to leave their seats in the front. The Pick-up had a separate driver's seat and a bench seat for two passengers, an arrangement which was offered as an extra-cost option on all other models. Panelvans came with two separate seats with either a walkway to the load

Padded sun visors and vinyl headlining with small perforations were fitted to all models, although Panelvans and Kombis lacked a full headlining in the rear. Manually operated sliding steel sunroof came as standard on luxury Microbuses – although this model could be ordered without one – and as an extra-cost option on other models.

vans and Pick-ups there is also a black-painted handle to assist in closing the cab door, and this is bolted into position immediately below the opening latches. In front of the latches, the window winders – the window glass was no longer of the sliding variety – have black plastic knobs and escutcheons, and steel winding arms with a black finish.

Microbuses have the luxury of large armrests on the interior cab door panels, and the grab handle below the opening finger latch is made of a softer, flexible material with chromed fixing lugs at each end. Luxury Microbuses have two-tone interior panels throughout to match the seats, the darker tones being used top and bottom, the lighter ones in the middle with the armrests trimmed to match. To lock and unlock the cab doors, a small black plastic push-pull button, identical to the contemporary Beetle type, is fitted at the rear of each window sill on all models except the Luxury Microbus, which has a locking catch integral with each interior door handle.

Swivelling chromed quarterlights seated in black rubbers were standard on the Luxury version of the Microbus. To begin with the chromed opening finger latches were small, elegant items that simply pushed forward to release the glass from the closed position. Beautifully made and durable, the only problem with these was that they were easily released from outside by a screwdriver, and they were therefore changed in August 1968 to the more familiar circular black plastic latches, which require a twisting movement before being pushed forward to release the window. Unfortunately, these plastic knobs have a tendency to break off, leaving the chromed metal latch beneath exposed and difficult to operate; replacement knobs are available but they never seem to last very long. Other models had fixed quarterlights or opening ones as an extra-cost option. Further quarterlights – up to three in all – were available as extra-cost options for the rear side windows, except for the one behind the sliding side door; an opened quarterlight here would have been knocked by the door.

A transversely ribbed rubber mat was fitted over the cab floor, and, although hard wearing, has a tendency to split in old age. Replacements are available, but not all are to the original pattern. All models have swivelling padded sun visors covered in white vinyl to match the headlining, and the Microbus L has a vanity mirror on the underside of the visor on the passenger's side. The rectangular rear-view mirror is much larger than the neat oval one on the Split-screens. From August 1970, the mirror body was made of black plastic, and the whole unit, now of the dipping variety, was intended to snap away from its retaining bracket in the event of an accident – yet another safety feature.

The cab's courtesy light is in the centre of the roof panel towards the rear of the compartment, and operates automatically with switches in the lower A pillar; the light also has a manual switch. Coat hooks made of soft plastic were provided across the range and fitted on the B pillars at the back of the cab. Again on a safety theme, the top of the dashboard is padded and covered in a non-reflective black vinyl.

In the rear compartment there are several differences between the models, but the basic layout is always the same. As before, the 'entry-level' people carrier, the Kombi, doubles as a load carrier by the simple expedient of undoing the retaining wing nuts – 10 in all – and removing the seats. Microbus seats can also be removed, but few customers went to the extra expense of buying a Microbus to do this and carry cargo instead.

Microbuses and Kombis came in standard form as eight-seaters with two cab seats, and two rows of three-seater benches in the rear compartment, the central bench having a tilting backrest for the seat nearest the side door. However, a two-seater bench in the centre (making the vehicle a seven-seater) could be ordered as an option. On the rare occasions when a second sliding door was ordered as an option, both ends of the central three-seater bench had tilting backrests. With the optional two-seater passenger bench in the cab as well, the vehicle became a nine-seater. The Double-cab Pick-up has the same three-seater arrangement in the front of the cab as the Single-cab model, but with a three-seater bench for rear passengers with additional luggage space and a heater outlet below it. These factory models should not be confused with Camper conversions, most of which have different seat configurations.

Kombis and Microbuses have a black rubber mat on the floor of the rear compartment. The Panelvan

Some Microbus comforts were added to the Pick-up, including vinyl headlining and padded sun visors, but vinyl seats and simple door panels (without heater ducting to rear, of course, but also with window-sill locking button and lacking an armrest) came only in single colours. Note position of courtesy light, and alloy chassis plate on rear wall.

went without one, although a good many owners fitted a mat as an afterthought when the paint on the floor chipped off and rust started bubbling. The Microbus L is distinguished from the regular version by having hard-wearing haircord carpet over the rear luggage compartment, so owners of other models also fitted similar carpets purchased from main dealers.

Panelvans have no interior panels on the side door and sides of the bodywork as there was no need for them, but Kombis and Microbuses have these panels and, in the case of the latter, they match those fitted to the cab doors. Kombi side panels, like those in the rear compartment of the Double-cab Pick-up, are rather crude pieces of fibreboard with concealed screw fixings to the metalwork. Microbuses have thickly padded armrests for passengers sitting on the

outside of the seats, and two alloy mouldings attached to the side panels for decoration. Microbuses also have vinyl-covered panels on the vertical pieces, or bulk-heads, behind the cab seats that create a walkway to the rear compartment.

Housed vertically on the rear left-hand side of the luggage compartment, the spare wheel on standard vehicles is exposed on Panelvans and Kombis, but covered in a vinyl glove on Microbuses. If the optional two-seater passenger bench and full-width cab parti-tion was fitted, the spare wheel was placed horizon-tally below the seat, freeing a little more luggage space at the rear.

The heating system provides vents in the cab's front panel, defrosting vents at the base of the windscreen, and rear compartment vents below the rear seat. In standard form Kombis and Panelvans were not provided with a heater in the rear compartment, but ducting was fitted so that a heater could be rigged up by dealers as an extra-cost option. Also as an extra-cost option (except on Single-cab and wide-bed Pick-ups), the infamous Eberspächer petrol heater could be fitted but relatively few Transporters had one. Although a good idea in principle, the Ebers-pächer runs off the main fuel system and requires a separate exhaust pipe, but it was amazingly expensive and rarely worked as well as it should have. Interesting as they are, these heaters are best avoided.

Additional items in the Microbus L include two chromed window bars around the perimeter of the rear luggage compartment to which luggage could be strapped, and three coat hooks – one behind the sliding door and two on the opposite side – above passengers' heads. An electrically-heated rear window

and a fully padded dashboard were also extra-cost options on all Microbuses. A steel sliding sunroof was standard on the Microbus L, but an extra-cost option on the Kombi and ordinary Microbus.

One source of irritation to owners of British and European Transporters is that a glovebox lid was not fitted as standard except on the Microbus L, although American-spec Transporters had one across the range. As a result glovebox lids have become rare, sought-after and relatively expensive to buy.

Like the one in the cab, the rear courtesy light is rectangular in shape, has a manual override switch, and is positioned towards the rear of the passenger compartment in line with the cab light. Both courtesy lights have opaque lenses. Three black plastic flexible grab handles for rear passengers – one behind the sliding door and two on the opposite side – are fitted in Microbuses of the late 1970s.

In addition to the ashtray in the centre of the dash-

board, there is an additional one in black plastic fitted to the bulkhead behind the driver for the benefit (or detriment) of rear passengers. This is bottom-hinged, pulls out from the top and, according to the Volkswagen brochure, was rather fancifully described as having been 'designed by a smoker for a smoker'. The meaning of this amusing phrase must be one of Volkswagen's most closely guarded secrets, because no-one known to me has ever fathomed it out.

The whole point of Volkswagen's efforts with the Bay-window Transporter's interior was to create an illusion. The design brief was to make it as similar to a comfortable passenger car as possible, a concept that was far removed from perceptions of other similar vehicles. Because it was so well thought out, it was well-received and, as a result, it received few major changes except by Camper specialists, who never ran out of ideas for making more attractive 'widgetry'.

As Volkswagen's advertising noted in 1970: 'People

Trim permutations between models and markets became more complex in the Bay-window era. This US-spec 1970 Microbus has neither two-tone seats nor bright trim strips on the side panels, but exterior waistline chrome strip would be a de luxe feature on European versions; seats can be found with transverse or longitudinal pleating, vinyl with plain or 'dog-tooth' pattern.

During the 1970 model year, Microbus spare wheel was moved to below front passenger bench except on vehicles with a walkway between cab seats (this feature was an extra-cost option on Panelvans and Kombis ordered with a full-width partition). The result was extra luggage space in the rear. Non-metric markets had speedometer marked to 90mph instead of 140kph. Volkswagen deserved a black mark for not providing a clock as standard on all vehicles; normally only the Microbus de luxe had one.

liked our idea so much that by 1967 we were producing 810 Transporters per day. A pretty impressive figure. And today, 1092 come off the assembly lines every 24 hours. With this sort of experience behind it, it's no wonder that the VW Commercial is the most popular commercial in the world.'

Apart from dropping the 'Clipper' name and replacing it with 'Microbus', nothing changed through 1968 and 1969 – except that the dealer

network was expanded to 5459 workshops in Europe and 8754 world-wide. In 1968 Volkswagen was busy with the launch of the Type 4 saloon and, naturally, the Transporter took a back-seat role.

From the 1971 model year the Kombi's interior side and door panels began to differ more significantly between one market and another, and there were many permutations. Some had armrests on all seats in the rear compartment, and some had the Luxury Microbus's decorative alloy mouldings fitted to vinyl-covered panels. It is usually safe to assume that a Kombi with these modifications today probably had them fitted as original equipment from new.

Interestingly, the official brochure for the 1971 model year lists for the first time a warning triangle among the accessories available at extra cost, a sign of how safety-conscious the motoring world had become at this time. Also for the 1971 model year, the driver's seat was modified so that it could be adjusted to 81 different positions, and the backrests of the cab seats were reshaped to give better lateral support. Again on a safety theme, vinyl-covered head restraints became available for the cab seats as extra-cost options for the 1972 model year, except on Panelvans with a dividing wall between cab and cargo compartment.

For the 1973 model year, Volkswagen offered a 12-seater Kombi for some markets (but never in Germany), and it proved especially popular with taxi firms. The layout comprises the driver's seat and two-seater bench in the cab (with the spare wheel horizontally positioned under this bench), a four-seater bench at the rear of the passenger compartment, a three-seater bench in the middle section, and two fold-away individual seats bolted to the vertical bulkhead behind the cab seats. The fold-aways are attached to the bulkhead with two tubular frames under each seat, which are hinged to allow the squabs to be flipped up when not in use. Passengers who occupy these useful seats face the rear of the vehicle. To improve access to the passenger compartment, a sliding door was fitted on each side and, as this was intended to be a 'no frills' omnibus, the seat material is in plain vinyl, or leatherette as Volkswagen chose to describe it, and has recessed buttons except in the cab upholstery. The bench seat in the centre of the vehicle also has cut-away shoulder pieces to expose part of the tubular seat framework to act as a grab handle. As the majority of these vehicles led hard lives, they too are comparatively rare today.

Incidentally, Volkswagen's sales literature for the 1973 model year listed no fewer than 28 'extras at no extra charge'. As the list included such items as a passenger grab handle on the dashboard, a feature that had been present from the beginning, it was little more than a 'puff' that fooled few.

Nothing much changed in August 1973, except that a cab parcel shelf was offered as an extra-cost option and Microbus owners could order the luxury of a tinted windscreen and a folding rear-seat

With separate cab seats – fitted with optional head restraints on this regular Microbus (above and left) – and a walkway to the rear, it is much easier to control unruly passengers. This 1974 vehicle has optional automatic transmission. Note armrest on central two-seater bench, a 'delete option' in place of standard three-seater bench, and rear compartment air vents (fed by the 'door tubes' that connect to circular ducts on the outer ends of the dashboard) on padded backs of 'walk-through' bulkhead. A larger steering wheel with wider spokes appeared in August 1977 and instrument design was simplified. This is a Panelvan, so no clock; additional switchgear operates auxiliary lamps.

The Kombi is a most versatile model. As in Split-screen period, central bench is secured by wing nuts, allowing it to be removed easily – or even fitted to face backwards.

backrest. In August 1974 the Luxury Microbus received black-coloured sun visors.

By 1975, Volkswagen could go little further in improving the interior. To do so would have required a major re-think about the vehicle's purpose and role. Increasing equipment levels would also have had the detrimental effect of taking up space, and one reason why so many people bought Transporters was because of their inherently roomy interiors.

INSTRUMENTS & CONTROLS

By the mid-1960s almost every car in the world had a comprehensive array of dashboard instruments and controls even if, in some cases, they were not strictly necessary. The exceptions were the People's Cars, namely the Beetle, the Citroën 2CV and the Mini.

Where the Beetle is concerned, Volkswagen made a concerted effort to keep everything as simple as possible, despite constant criticism from journalists that a single instrument – the combined speedometer and fuel gauge – was incongruously austere in an increasingly sophisticated age. Volkswagen took the view that the Beetle was selling well and was, therefore, to be left well alone. On the other hand, the company's policy towards other models in the range – the Type 3, Type 4, Karmann-Ghia and second-generation Transporter – was altogether different.

Like the Beetle, the Split-screen Transporter had a simple dashboard layout which, historically and philosophically, was absolutely correct, but from its inception the Bay-window followed the Type 3 and 4 saloons in having a much revised and more modern facia panel. As the advertising literature stated, 'the new VW Commercial has a new instrument panel to give you genuine finger-tip control'. By and large this claim was perfectly true, apart from the floor-mounted straight gear lever which, being 4cm (1.6in) longer than the one fitted to the Split-screens, was

considerably more vague in action. And journalists pulled no punches in criticising it.

World Car Guide in 1968 commented: 'Now that Hirst and others have introduced positive action Beetle shifters, we suggest that they devote their attention to the Bus, as finding reverse is kind of like the old party game of pinning a tail on the donkey. The criticism evaporates once you're in gear, however, as the clutch action in the Bus is undoubtedly the sweetest ever to be put into a car.'

Immediately in front of the driver the three circular spaces for instruments are deeply recessed – to prevent reflections from the windscreen – in a rectangular, plastic 'crackle' finish panel that is secured to the facia with a Phillips screw in each corner. All the instruments were made and supplied by VDO, and have white characters on a background of grey with a pale centre (early vehicles) or all-black (late

Despite unrestored history and nearly 170,000kms on the clock, 1978 Kombi's remarkable cab interior remains in 'as-new' condition. Cab step is protected by a rubber covering, while door trim shows late style with air vents and black fittings.

Considerably less luxurious than the Microbus, Kombi had unpleated upholstery with 'dog-tooth' grain, and roof panel and window areas were untrimmed. Luggage compartment had no carpeting in standard form.

vehicles). Calibrated to 90mph or 140kph, the speedometer includes a distance counter and sits in the centre of the cluster flanked by an electric fuel gauge on the left and a 'blank' on the right.

This 'blank' was typically German and totally absurd. On Luxury Microbuses a clock was fitted here as standard – an extra-cost option on other models – but charging for this feature, which was clearly unnecessary on account of the wrist-watch having been invented many years earlier, did not go down well with customers. With the engine sited so far away from the driver, and not especially audible in the cab, the Transporter was crying out for a tachometer but it never got one.

Warning lights for the generator, oil pressure, headlamp high beam, parking lights and indicators are housed in the lower segment of the fuel gauge. Inboard of the 'blank' (or clock) are four slide controls which operate vertically to control the ventilation and heating system. The plastic finger knobs are roughly square and finished in red for warm air and blue for cold air. The vents under the rear bench seat are controlled by levers on the vents themselves. Under the front of the driver's seat is a further plastic pull-knob for releasing extra heat into the vents in the front panel.

In the centre of the dashboard was a blanking plate that had to be removed if a radio was installed – and most customers chose one. The radio speaker sits below the centre of the dashboard. Directly below the radio position is a sliding ashtray with a padded lid featuring the 'H' gearchange pattern. Below the ashtray, the push-pull type handbrake lever has a black plastic handle.

Where a glovebox lid was fitted, it has a black plastic turning knob, but this was dropped in August 1974 in favour of a raised finger grip on the bottom edge. At each end of the dashboard is a swivelling circular vent for directing fresh air and heat into the cabin. Further vents on the lower part of the front panel direct cold or warm air to ankle level. In August 1971 the ventilation and heating systems were further improved when louvred air outlets were fitted in the front doors in order to extract air out through slots.

Switchgear on the dashboard's bottom bar comprises a pull knob outboard of the steering column for operating the interior courtesy lights, and similar knobs inboard of the column for the headlamps, windscreen wipers and hazard warning lights. All knobs are in soft non-reflective black plastic and feature white identity symbols.

The indicator stalk, initially a chromed lever with a slim black plastic finger grip, is on the left of the steering column, and also operates the headlamp dipswitch and headlamp flasher when pulled forwards. For the 1972 model year, the windscreen wiper/washer switch was transferred and operated by a stalk on the right-hand side of the steering column. At the same time, both stalks were made of plastic and given white identity symbols. The top of the dashboard is generously padded and covered in vinyl with a textured finish. Where the top bar crosses the instrument panel, it is raised to form a shroud to further prevent reflections from the windscreen.

The steering wheel was a dished two-spoker in black plastic with a horn button at the centre. A revised wheel, with a substantially thicker rim and spokes, was introduced in August 1977.

ELECTRICS

All Bay-window models were fitted with 12-volt electrics, the vast majority of components from Bosch. The 12-volt 45Ah battery – made by Bosch or Volkswagen – sits in the same position as on the Split-screen models, and is secured by metal clamps on the right-hand side of the engine compartment. The system is negatively earthed. In August 1971 a computer diagnostic socket was fitted in the engine compartment and, as a result, the battery gained a small lead which senses the level of electrolyte.

As before, the dynamo is mounted on a detachable alloy pedestal on the right-hand half of the crankcase, and is belt-driven from the crankshaft pulley. The engine's cooling fan is attached directly to the nose of the dynamo's armature shaft. The voltage regulator and cut-out unit were remote-mounted, behind the air cleaner. The dynamo's outer casing was made of alloy as previously and had a natural 'satin' finish. This has a tendency to corrode and also picks up a good deal of grime but, with the regulator out of harm's way, it is a good deal easier to keep clean.

The 0.7hp starter motor, of slightly greater output than on the old six-volters, is housed on the top right-hand side of the gearbox and was made either by Bosch or Volkswagen. Entirely conventional, switching and engagement is by solenoid, the pinion being driven through a roller clutch. From August 1971, the starter motor was also wired to the fault diagnostic system. Starter motors fitted to models with automatic transmission differ from manuals: because the torque converter requires more power to fire it into life, the starter is rated at 0.8hp, and has copper instead of aluminium field coils and two brushes instead of four. Generally, these more powerful starter motors were also made by Bosch.

Situated under the dashboard, the two-speed windscreen wiper motor is bolted to a frame attached to the bodywork under the dashboard itself. The motor is simple in that it contains a shaft which engages with a gear that turns a common crank; this in turn operates the long wiper blades. From August 1971 the wiring to and from the wiper motor was neatly encased in a plug, so that the motor and frame could be removed without having to disconnect all the wiring separately. The plastic washer bottle is attached to the body via a bracket behind the front panel trim in the cab. The fusebox is also fitted in a console under the dashboard; initially there were just eight fuses, extended to 10 in August 1968 and finally 12 from August 1970.

The 12-volt headlamps were an improvement over the pitiful six-volt units, and shone with something approaching a white, rather than a dreary yellow, light. European-spec headlamps were fitted with 45/40-watt bulbs while American-spec sealed-beam units had 50/40-watt items. The other bulbs were rated as follows: indicators, 21-watt; stop and tail lamps, 21/5-watt; number plate lamp, 10-watt; reversing lights, 25-watt; interior courtesy lights, 10-watt; parking light, 4-watt; dashboard warning lights, 1.2-watt. The heated rear screen (where fitted) was rated as 60-watt.

Mounted on a bracket under the left-hand front wing, the Bosch horn is not interchangeable with the one fitted to the Split-screen. Although it is more powerful, the 12-volt horn still managed to make the same uninspiring tone, something along the lines of a sleepy, flatulent, bovine sound. Most Volkswagen drivers appear to be very polite road users because they are just too embarrassed by the noise of the horn to actually use it.

Attached by a single bracket to the left-hand side of the fan housing, the coil was a black, plastic-bodied Bosch item which, like its six-volt counterpart, is rarely fitted today, as the more powerful Blue Bosch coil is altogether more satisfactory. Bosch also made and supplied the distributor, which is bolted to the top left-hand side of the crankcase, fitted with automatic advance and retard, and has conventional contact breaker points with a gap of 0.4mm.

After August 1973 an electronic device was fitted to the distributor for the purpose of establishing the position of top dead centre – essential in timing the ignition – more accurately. The automatic advance and retard mechanism works in a conventional manner with a centrifugal governor fitted in the distributor. The governor's weights move outwards as engine speed increases, which forces the cam to turn and advance the ignition. Springs attached to the governor pull the weights when engine speed is reduced, and the cam returns to its 'normal' position. The vacuum control bellows is situated on the side of the distributor body.

The electronic fault diagnosis system fitted to all Transporters from August 1971 takes the form of a multi-pin socket in the top left-hand side of the engine compartment. When linked to a dealer's computer, the system was capable of diagnosing up to 86 potential faults during each 6000-mile service. The system works well provided there are no faults with the vehicle's wiring, and acts as an *aide memoire* for mechanics. With the inevitable increase in wiring demanded by this system, electrical repairs are necessarily more time consuming. Vehicles fitted with this system had a sticker in the engine compartment displaying a computer diagnostic number.

In August 1973 the trusty dynamo, which had seen service virtually unchanged in principle since Beetle production began in 1945, was swapped for an alternator, the advantage being that an alternator is able to dispense a higher current at low engine speeds, and keep the battery topped up with 'juice' irrespective of engine speed. And although it has a voltage regulator – normally built-in but sometimes remote-mounted next to the battery – there is no cut-out device as the current only travels in one direction. Driven by a belt from the crankshaft pulley, the alternator runs at an engine speed/alternator speed ratio of 1:2.26.

ENGINE

Because the Bay-window is so much heavier than the vehicle it replaced, it was crying out for more power, not that Volkswagen were going to throw caution to the wind and replace the trusty 1500 single-port engine with a real fire-breather. Instead, they stayed with the same air-cooled flat-four design, but increased its size from 1493cc (91.11cu in) to 1584cc

To the same design as the 1500, 1600 engine offered more power, but it was still woefully inadequate by comparison with American rivals. This example is still fitted with an original black coil. Distributor, with externally mounted vacuum mechanism, sits to left of mechanically driven fuel pump and detachable alloy dynamo pedestal. As ever, engine number is stamped into crankcase below dynamo pedestal.

(96.66cu in) with a bore and stroke of 85.5mm × 69.0mm (3.37in × 2.72in). Known popularly as 'The Sixteen', the new engine produced a maximum 47bhp at 4000rpm.

Through this 1600 era, life for the engineers became a little more complex. As before the engine number was stamped on the crankcase directly below the dynamo, or generator, pedestal, and prefixed by a letter, or letters: B indicates an early 47bhp engine unit with or without emissions control; AD denotes a 50bhp engine, which was installed for the 1971 model year; AE is the same as AD but with emissions control; and AF indicates a low-compression engine with a compression ratio of 6.6:1 rather than the normal 7.7:1. Low-compression engines were generally supplied to countries where the fuel was not usually up to European or North American grades.

Inevitably, it is important that your vehicle is fitted with the correct serial number and type of power unit when restoring a Transporter to its original factory condition. Engines without a serial number are usually, but not always, reconditioned exchange units.

The basic Beetle configuration was used for the new 1600 engine, but the Transporter followed Type 3 saloon practice in having a two-point cross-member mounting at the rear end to provide improved support for the engine and give improved resistance to torque and vibration. Unlike the Type 3, however, which had its cooling fan mounted on the nose of the crankshaft, the Transporter retained the Beetle's fan housing mounted vertically on top of the crankcase.

With four opposed cylinders, the magnesium-alloy crankcase is split vertically into two halves and bolted together. The short crankshaft, which was made much stronger for the new engine, runs in aluminium alloy shell bearings located between the two halves of the crankcase. The four cast iron cylinder barrels are finned to aid cooling, and fit into circular apertures cast integrally with the crankcase. Each pair of barrels shares an alloy cylinder head attached to the barrels by long threaded studs screwed into the crankcase on their inner ends and bolted to the cylinder heads at their opposite ends. The cylinder heads were to the same design as those on the 1500 engines, and both the 'Fifteen' and 'Sixteen' heads were slightly larger versions of the previous 1200 version.

The pushrods are located at the camshaft end in flat-faced cylindrical cam followers, as on previous engines built after May 1959, and run through pushrod tubes – these notoriously leak oil – to the rocker gear in the cylinder heads, which at this stage were still of the trusty single-port variety. The combustion chambers are roughly wedge-shaped, the shape being determined by the cylinder heads, and the flat-topped Mahle pistons (or concave in the case of low-compression engines) are made of alloy and have two compression rings and one oil scraper ring. To a conventional design, the connecting rods are forged, and the piston gudgeon pins are fully floating and held in position by circlips.

Bolted to the top of the left-hand crankcase, the distributor is shaft-driven from a gear on the rear of the crankshaft. A cam on this shaft also operates the fuel pump (to the right of the distributor) operating rod. Housed at the rear of the crankcase, the gear-type oil pump is driven by a horizontal shaft operated by a tongue-and-slot arrangement on the camshaft. At what Volkswagen people generally describe as the front of the engine, the flywheel is located on the crankshaft with four dowel pegs and secured to it by a large, central bolt which houses needle roller bearings for the gearbox input shaft.

As the engine does not have a conventional sump, the oil does not pass through a conventional filter. There is, however, a removable gauze filter at the bottom of the crankcase, access to which is through a strainer plate. The engine's cooling system, which is regulated by a bellows-type thermostat under the right-hand pair of cylinders, depends as much on oil as it does on air for cooling, which is why the vertical oil cooler is mounted on the left-hand side of the crankcase close to the cooling fan.

The cooling fan draws air from outside and blows it over the oil cooler, cylinder heads and barrels, and the spent hot air is emitted under the rear valance. Hot air is also utilised by the heat exchangers – integral parts of the exhaust system – to provide heat for the cabin. For restorers today it is well worth investing in genuine Volkswagen heat exchangers; they are expensive but pattern parts generally do not have the same thermo-dynamic properties, resulting in comparatively little heat finding its way into the interior. Naturally, the same sort of narrow-bore inlet manifold was used, but the inlet and exhaust valve diameters were increased respectively to 35.6mm (1.40in) and 32.1mm (1.26in) to help the 1600 engine breathe more efficiently.

As before, Solex was the favoured carburettor supplier and there were several types – 30 PICT 1, 30 PICT 2, 30 PICT 3 and 34 PICT 3 – which differ in the minutest detail according to market. All are of the single-choke downdraught type, fitted with an automatic choke and an electro-magnetic cut-off valve to prevent fuel getting into the manifold and causing overrunning when the engine is hot. PICT 1 (not fitted to American-spec models) and PICT 2 (American-spec only) have just two adjuster screws for the throttle stop and volume control, PICT 3 has an additional air by-pass screw, and 34 PICT 3 has an angled pilot jet position. Unlike the Split-screen models, the carburettors fitted to Bay-windows are without throttle governors.

The PICT 2, fitted to vehicles exported to North America, has a larger float bowl, larger oil-bath air cleaner, different jets and emissions control. This carburettor was designed to deliver the fuel/air mixture to the combustion chambers more accurately with the result that the distributor has a different advance curve and dashpot. Vacuum-controlled from the inlet manifold, the dashpot holds the throttle slightly open during deceleration, so that just enough fuel is allowed through and, therefore, burns more effectively and cleanly. With 0 degree timing at top dead centre and a comparatively low idle speed on other engines, emissions were kept to a minimum. Recommended sparking plugs for the 1600 were Bosch W145 T1, Beru 145/14 or Champion L884.

Volkswagen also took further steps to prevent the age-old problem of carburettor 'icing' in cold weather, which had always been an inherent result of using such a long-travel inlet manifold. Twin carburettors with one short manifold apiece would have been the easiest solution to this perennial malady, but Volkswagen instead fitted a revised valve in the air cleaner connected to a thermostat by a cable. The valve closes when the engine is cold and allows warm air from the right-hand heat exchanger to the carburettor through a flexible card-type hose.

After the engine has warmed up, the valve opens and cool air flows into the carburettor. It is a simple system and, by and large, it works well insomuch that it helps to minimise the difference between the engine temperature and the fuel/air mixture. But the passage of many years has seen these Solexes gain something of a reputation for unreliability. In practice they are reasonably durable but, like all things mechanical, they do wear out, and such is the high cost of a professional overhaul – and DIY rebuilds are virtually out of the question – that many owners endure icing-up and all the other usual carburettor problems to the bitter end, or fit a cheap alternative.

Bay-window models have a larger fuel tank of 55 litres (12.1 Imperial gallons, 14.5 US gallons), although the official advertising literature claimed that it was 60 litres – an interesting and somewhat reassuring mistake.

Overall, the new 1600 engine was welcomed by Volkswagen enthusiasts because of its extra power. Although the top speed of 65mph (105kph) was still nothing to write home about, the Transporter was never intended to be a performance machine. Most owners also quickly cottoned on to the indisputable fact that the true top speed was in excess of 70mph (113kph), and the 'Wednesday afternoon' vehicle – as opposed to those that were manufactured on a Monday morning – would give close on 80mph (128kph) performance.

The 1600 engine was also reliable, which can be largely attributed to the fact that, from the beginning of Bay-window production, the crankcase was made stronger and had improved, more efficient oilways. These power units always felt smooth, were largely fuss-free, and improved vastly after bedding in properly, which usually took a minimum of 10,000 miles.

In August 1970, Volkswagen answered its critics of the past 20 years by modifying the cylinder heads to give them two inlet ports instead of one. This modification allowed the engine to breathe more efficiently and, as a bonus, power output at 4000rpm consequently increased from 47bhp to 50bhp.

By late 1960s exhaust emission regulations in North America dictated significant changes to carburettor settings and air filter arrangement.

With the benefit of hindsight, this modification was not one of Volkswagen's best. These heads quickly developed a reputation for cracking, and for no good reason other than that the metal between the two ports was necessarily thin; with prolonged, hard use the considerable heat build-up was prone to causing damage in all sorts of unlikely places. This, however, was not everyone's experience, as there are thousands of twin-porters still regularly in use having never given a moment's trouble.

At the same time as the twin-port heads were introduced, the steel oil cooler was changed for a similar unit made of aluminium alloy to help dissipate heat more efficiently, and it was also positioned at an angle instead of being upright as previously. As a result the ducting 'tinware' at the front of the engine was modified to pass a greater volume of cooling air to the oil cooler via the fan, which was also enlarged.

The other component that was modified as a result of the introduction of twin-port heads was, naturally, the inlet manifold. As before this branches from a single pipe directly below the carburettor for a short distance before dividing into two. Before reaching the heads, the new arrangement included a beautifully cast, alloy double-pipe manifold between the steel manifold and heads. These were separate pieces and joined on their inner edge to the single-pipe mani-fold via rubber washers and steel clips, and with bolts

to the heads on their outer ends. Being made of alloy these pieces can, of course, be polished almost to a mirror finish, and several concours entrants have gone down this road, but the factory made them with a natural, rough-cast finish – and this is what concours judges want to see these days.

For August 1971, when Beetle sales were peaking and the Transporter had become the 'People's number one commercial' in just about every country where it was sold, Volkswagen made something of an engine transplant. Whereas the Pick-up truck soldiered on with the 1600 engine, the other models in the range were fitted optionally with the 1700 engine that had first seen service in Volkswagen's relatively unsuc-cessful Type 4 saloon launched in 1968. In the US all models, including the Pick-up, were fitted with this power unit.

Although the 1700 was virtually the same as all previous engines in principle and layout, there were detail differences. Referred to in Volkswagen lore as the 'suitcase' engine, the 1700 had its cooling fan moved from the top of the engine and fitted on the nose of the crankshaft at the rear, making for a most compact unit. The cooling fan itself was contained within a new type of housing which, apart from making components like the sparking plugs even more difficult to change, conducts air over the engine in a guided arrangement of ducts. In theory this

allows for more efficient cooling, and was more in line with what Porsche had been doing on its range of sports and sports racing cars.

With a bore and stroke of 90mm × 60mm (3.54in × 2.36in), the revised engine displaced 1679cc (102.46cu in) and developed 66bhp at 4800rpm. Oil capacity was increased from 2.5 litres (4.5 pints) to 3.5 litres (6.125 pints), as the crankcase had been completely reworked for improved lubrication and yet larger oilways. The crankshaft bearings were also improved with lead-coated aluminium being used for numbers 1, 2 and 3 and a three-layer, steel-backed material for number 4. The camshaft shell bearings, however, continued to be made of white metal with steel backings. Valve diameters were increased too, the inlet to 39.3mm (1.55in) and the exhaust to 33.0mm (1.30in). Because this engine is heavier than the previous units, it is secured to the gearbox with eight bolts and nuts rather than four as previously.

The biggest shock to Volkswagen enthusiasts upon the launch of the 1700 was that, at last, here was an air-cooled flat-four with twin carburettors – a brace of beautiful Solex 34 PDSITs – fitted on top of short-

travel manifolds which, at one fell swoop, solved the icing-up problem in cold weather. As a result of these modifications, there were other detail changes which, at first glance, appear relatively unimportant but need to be taken into account during restoration work.

Because of the new cooling fan, the cooling tinware was altered in shape and is not interchangeable with previous models, and the new carburettors demanded the use of a revised air filter. The latter is a large, ugly affair of the oil element species, which sits across the top of the crankcase and has flat, ribbed induction pipes leading to each carburettor from its sides. Access to its inside is via a removable top held in place by spring clips. The exhaust system was also changed, both the heat exchangers and heavy tailbox being altered in shape with a single tail-pipe exiting on the left-hand side. When it comes to changing the exhaust system, expect plenty of grief, both financially and gymnastically – they are absolute pigs both to remove and fit.

In June 1972 *Car* magazine carried out a comprehensive road test on the 1700 and reckoned it to be 'streets ahead' of the earlier 1500 and 1600 models in performance. The 1700 was some 8sec faster over the quarter mile at 21.4sec and top speed was up to 76mph. At a constant 60mph the writer of the test also found an improvement in fuel economy, up to 22.7mpg compared with the magazine's 1968 test on the 1600 at 17.3mpg. The new model was also found to be capable of taking a 1-in-16 gradient in top gear compared to the old model's best of 1-in-22. *Car* made the point that the 1700 engine 'transforms the vehicle's performance, giving it real punch through the gears, a quite respectable top speed, and sound cruising ability'.

In August 1973, Volkswagen introduced the 1800 engine in an attempt to give the Transporter a little

Distinguishable by cast alloy inlet manifold, twin-port cylinder heads were introduced in August 1970. They helped the engine to 'breathe' more freely and raised power output from 47bhp to 50bhp. Into the electronic age, a computer diagnostic socket (left) was fitted in the engine compartment from August 1971.

Suddenly the Transporter engine looked very different. Similar to the unit fitted to the Type 4 saloon, Volkswagen's compact 1700 'suitcase' engine was optionally offered (except for Pick-ups) from August 1971. Twin Solex carburettors eradicated the perennial problem of 'icing' in cold weather. A useful inspection hatch (right) was introduced with the 'suitcase' engine to allow easier access for servicing and maintenance.

more power. The increase in capacity was obtained by widening the bore from 90mm (3.54in) to 93mm (3.66in) giving an overall capacity of 1795cc (109.5cu in). One of the great advantages of an air-cooled engine is that an increase in capacity can be easily achieved by replacing the detachable cylinders with bigger ones, although the cylinder heads, of course, have to be enlarged. But in this case it is not easy to appreciate why Volkswagen bothered because the gain in power was a mere 2bhp. There was a useful gain in torque, however, which rose from 81lb ft at 3200rpm to 92.4lb ft at 3000rpm, and the vast majority of owners appreciated this especially on hills.

The 1800 engine was also treated to a number of other modifications. The walls of the cast iron cylinder barrels were made thicker in an attempt to maintain durability, because merely 'boring out' the 1700 would have left the walls perilously thin, as a number of tuning customisers have found to their cost. The inlet ports were slightly altered in shape, the combustion chambers were enlarged, and valve diameters were slightly increased to 41mm (1.61in) inlet and 34mm (1.34in) exhaust. As a result of the slight increase in power, the clutch springs were strengthened, and the oil-bath air cleaner was replaced by a more modern unit fitted with a paper element.

During this period Volkswagen had become Europe's largest motor manufacturer. Even by American standards the company was a giant, and inevitably it became embroiled in producing vehicles that differed markedly one to the next to suit legislation

in various export markets. Not even Volkswagen knows how many different permutations there were of the Transporter by 1975, but it was certainly well into five figures. So, when it comes to ignition timing, for example, it is essential to consult an official manual for a particular model before starting work, as there are differences between them.

Generally, European-spec engines with a P prefix need to be timed at 17.5 degrees before TDC, American-spec engines with an S prefix (automatic gearbox) at 10 degrees after TDC, and American-spec engines with an N prefix (manual gearbox) at 5 degrees after TDC. Different sparking plugs were also recommended for different climates. For Europe Bosch W145 T2, Beru 145/14/3 or Champion N88 were best, whereas Transporters exported to tropical countries had Bosch W175 T2 or Beru 175/14/3.

Despite such a small gain in performance over the 1700 engine, journalists considered the 1800 to be worthwhile. The South African journal, *Car*, noted the enhanced torque levels and commented, 'it clearly shows up in acceleration tests. While the automatic is fairly slow to get moving – even in 1800 form it

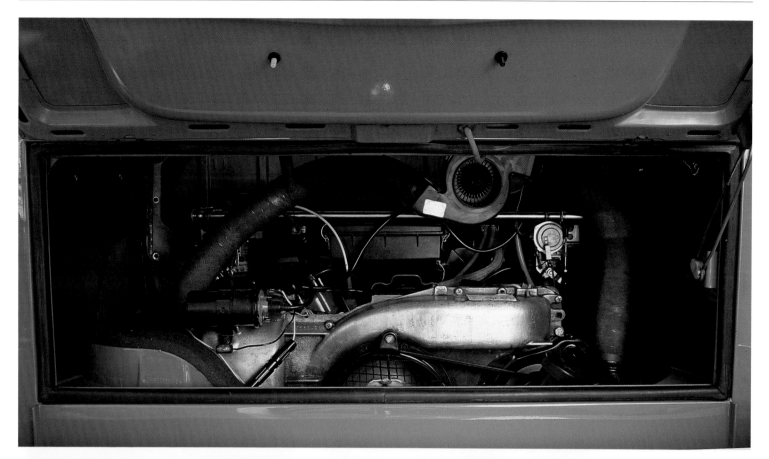

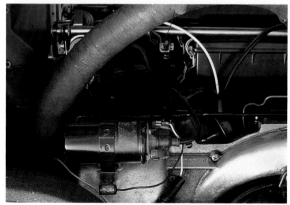

Following the 1700 and 1800 engines, the 2-litre, introduced in August 1975, was the largest air-cooled power unit ever produced by Volkswagen, endowing the Transporter with 90mph performance. With upright fan housing gone and cooling fan mounted on nose of crankshaft, coil was attached to alloy shroud (far left) and engine number was stamped immediately to its right. Replenishing oil became easier with 'suitcase' engine, as filler neck was placed separately at rear (left) instead of being cast into dynamo pedestal.

merely lifts its nose and then eases away from rest – the new model is about 30 per cent faster in the standard 0-100kph sprint.' Whereas the 1700's 0-100kph (0-62mph) time was 34.9sec, the figure for the 1800 was 25.8sec.

It was almost inevitable that, as the larger engine had to work less hard than the 1700 unit, it also had improved fuel consumption, the majority of owners managing to achieve 26mpg with sensible driving. Vehicles fitted with automatic gearboxes were slightly worse at around 24mpg.

While the 1700 was superseded by the 1800, the trusty 1600 model was offered as an alternative, even after the introduction of the final incarnation of the air-cooled engine, the 2-litre in August 1975. This was the largest air-cooled flat-four Volkswagen ever made and, like the 1700 and 1800 was, regrettably, never fitted to the Beetle. In many respects the 2-litre was a brilliant engine: I clearly recall a trip as a passenger in a 2-litre vehicle on an English motorway for many

miles at highly illegal speeds in the outside lane, overtaking just about everything in our path.

By the mid-1970s, however, similar vehicles from other manufacturers had just about caught up Volkswagen – and some had overtaken – and motoring journalists were at last becoming more critical of the Transporter. The South African *Car* magazine tested a 2-litre Microbus in 1978 and commented: 'The gain has been principally in acceleration and overtaking ability. There has also been a small gain in fuel economy with the 2-litre model owing to improved torque and gearing. But the 2-litre engine has not been an unqualified success: with its big pistons and long stroke, it feels more 'lomp' than earlier motors, and maximum speed has actually dropped.'

With this engine both the bore and stroke were increased to 84mm × 71mm (3.70in × 2.80in), giving a capacity of 1970cc (120.2cu in) and producing 70bhp at 4200rpm. As an aside, this was less power than Volkswagen extracted from its water-cooled

Traditional 1600 engine with upright cooling fan was offered as an alternative to more powerful 'suitcase' unit in lesser models until end of production – here it is seen in 1978 Kombi. Alternator replaced dynamo from 1973; note chassis number stamped into bodywork at bottom left.

1600cc engine less than a decade later. Little wonder, therefore, that the writing was on the wall for the faithful air-cooled unit by the mid-1970s. The 2-litre engine was in fact the same as the 1800, except for the obvious difference in bore and stroke dimensions – even the valve sizes were retained.

Twin Solex carburettors were replaced with fuel injection on the 1800 engine, but only for some markets such as North America and, at first, for California only (vehicles for California also had a carbon filter in the fuel tank to absorb fumes when the filler cap was removed). It is important to note that different prefix letters were given to the larger capacity engines, as follows: 1800 with carburettors (AW), 1800 with fuel injection (GD, GB). The fuel injection system was a Bosch AFC (air flow controlled) which comprises an electrically-operated fuel pump, an electrically-controlled computer unit and sensors, fuel injectors, fuel lines and induction manifolds. As it is a non-direct injection system, the fuel injectors spray fuel into the induction housings. There is a cold start valve that automatically ensures that the fuel/air mixture is correct for cold starting. A fuel filter is situated next to the electric fuel pump. Because the control unit is next to the battery, it is vulnerable to spilled electrolyte.

It goes without saying that twin Solex carburettors and fuel injection systems are highly complex, and require qualified mechanics to restore them to health should anything go wrong. Both systems are well beyond the scope of normal mortals, as setting them up properly requires special tools and equipment. The days when setting up a Solex properly by ear disappeared with the advent of twin carburettors.

TRANSMISSION

Volkswagen's all-synchromesh gearbox is renowned for its reliability and longevity but, because of its complexity, it must be considered a complete 'no-go' area for amateur restorers. Rebuilding one requires special tools and sound specialist knowledge. Rewiring a Boeing 747 by comparison is fairly straightforward.

The gearbox sits immediately in front of the engine, secured by four or eight bolts. At the front it is supported by bearers attached to the transverse torsion bar tube, and damped against vibration by a rubber mounting. As on the Split-screen, the engine-gearbox assembly is supported by a crossmember that runs directly under the gearbox. And, as before, the gearbox and final drive assembly is housed in a one-piece 'tunnel' type magnesium alloy casting ribbed for strength and to aid cooling. Drive from the engine to the gearbox is via a threaded input shaft.

With the majority of conventional gearboxes, and Volkswagen gearboxes could never be described as conventional, there is usually an input and an output shaft on the same axis, and a layshaft and gear wheels directly below them. However, the Bay-window's system utilises an input and output shaft alone, which sit side by side with both carrying a synchro hub. The output shaft incorporates the pinion which, in turn, meshes with the crownwheel.

The 200mm (7.87in) Fichtel & Sachs clutch is located in the gearbox bellhousing and operated by a cable, which runs from the foot pedal through the centre of the chassis to an operating lever on the top left-hand side of the gearbox casing. The cable is adjustable with a small wing nut secured to a flange on the operating lever. The clutch itself is a single dry-plate disc cushioned by coil springs up to August 1970 and a diaphragm thereafter.

One component with particularly painful memories for me is the clutch release thrust bearing, which fits over the input shaft and is released by the operating lever via a transverse fork roughly in the centre of the bellhousing. With age, use and abuse, both the bearing and the fork can wear out and break, and it pays, I assure you, to replace them with genuine Volkswagen parts, as many pattern parts are about as useful as the tissue paper in which they are wrapped.

A major modification that took place between the Split-screen and Bay-window models involves the design of the drive to the rear wheels. The former swing-axle system was considered by many, including Ralph Nader, to be inherently flawed. Under exceptionally hard cornering, the tendency of the swing axles to 'jack' themselves up caused the dreaded wheel 'tuck-in', and provoked allegedly uncontrollable quantities of oversteer. Seasoned campaigners who learned to drive Volkswagens properly know the Nader-inspired criticism to be absolute hogwash.

But, where the Transporter is concerned, the critics got their way. Volkswagen relented to pressure and came up with a new type of swinging axle similar to the design of contemporary Porsche 911s. The hub reduction gears were dropped altogether, which is a great advantage when it comes to rebuilds, and the old, heavy driveshafts were replaced by much smaller, slender shafts, whose sole role is to transmit drive from the gearbox to the rear wheels. Unlike the original swinging axles, they play no part in the suspension.

Articulation at both ends of each driveshaft is provided by universal joints. The wheels are supported on separate shafts that run in bearings on the longitudinal trailing arms. The splined driveshafts are coupled to the final drive unit and wheel shafts by flanges attached by cap screws. With the old swing axles, the driveshafts run in cylindrical tubes and are lubricated along with the wheel bearings by oil from the gearbox, but the driveshafts on Bay-windows need to be lubricated as part of the general service routine. To accomplish this the rubber gaiters on the inner and outer ends of the driveshafts need to be removed. Volkswagen specified lithium grease with molybdenum disulphide for this.

One great advantage of the revised system is that the driveshafts, gearbox and wheel bearings can be removed separately, which considerably reduces the time required for repairs. Many believe that the real advantage of what is often incorrectly referred to as the 'fully independent rear suspension' (the original swing-axle system is also independent) was an improvement in roadholding. Insomuch as the post-1967 Transporters have a tendency to understeer rather than oversteer, they are arguably safer in corners beyond the limit of tyre adhesion, but are

Unimaginatively styled shift lever for automatic transmission, available as an option from August 1972, has six different positions.

certainly a lot less fun and require a deal less skill from the driver.

For most owners the real benefit of the new transmission lay with the taller gearbox ratios, which are as follows: first, 3.80:1; second, 2.06:1; third, 1.26:1; fourth, 0.89:1; reverse, 3.61:1; final drive, 4.125:1. Fourth gear is so comparatively high that it equates to fifth gear on several passenger saloons of the 1970s and '80s, and was partially responsible for improving fuel consumption.

For markets where customers anticipated driving regularly on slippery road surfaces, Volkswagen offered a limited-slip differential as an extra-cost option. To a conventional design, the differential side gears are connected by a friction clutch, which slips in normal operating conditions to allow the driveshafts to perform their function. When the throttle pedal is pressed, irrespective of the road surface, the side gears and pinion separate, which allows the differential covers to be forced on the casing of the differential and lock it in place. As with so many limited-slip differential systems, the handling characteristics feel most odd to the uninitiated, and for those who need extra traction it is cheaper and simpler to carry a heavy load over the rear wheels.

From August 1972 all Transporters with the larger engine (the 1700 at that stage), except the Pick-up, came with the option of a three-speed automatic gearbox. Volkswagen had offered a semi-automatic 'box on the Beetle in 1968, but it proved to be unpopular, as did the similar unit employed on the 'Sportomatic' Porsche 911. The Transporter's fully automatic gearbox comprises a front casting housing the epicyclic train and oil pump, a rear casting containing the gears and final drive, and a torque converter situated within the bellhousing; the torque converter case is bolted to the flywheel. For those who appreciate the complexities of the manual gearbox, the automatic is a complete nightmare.

There are two turbine discs in the torque converter casing; one turns in the same direction as the engine and the other, which turns independently, is mounted on a splined shaft meshed to the driving gear in the gearbox itself. Turbine vanes are situated next to the flywheel, and it is from the turbine that drive goes to the planetary gears, and is carried from the epicyclic system via the pinion shaft. The pinion shaft is splined to the output gear of the gear train. Automatic transmission fluid is pumped around the torque converter and the transmission case of the epicyclic box, and transmits power to the torque converter as well as providing lubrication.

Hypoid gear oil is provided in a separate system for lubricating the final drive assembly. When the engine is switched on the torque converter casing rotates with the flywheel, and the transmission fluid is driven under pressure by the pump to the torque converter. The fluid is then driven by centrifugal force from an impeller into the turbine vanes. The turbine then turns and forces the fluid towards the impeller. It then comes into contact with the stator, or centre disc, that turns along with the impeller, which decreases the oil flow, increases its pressure through the turbine and consequently speeds up the turbine.

This is done by multiplying torque by a maximum factor of 2.5, but, as the turbine's speed increases to the point where it is equal to that of the impeller, fluid then flows readily through the stator, and torque decreases until the speed ratio between the turbine and impeller is exactly 0.84:1. When the torque created by the engine and turbine are equal to each other, the torque converter acts as a mere fluid coupling and not as a torque converter.

The shift lever has six different positions: P for parking, R for reverse, N for neutral, D for drive, 2 for 'second' (which prevents top gear being automatically selected at inappropriate times such as driving in heavy traffic), and 1 for 'first' (which is normally used in slow traffic or climbing and descending steep hills at low speeds). In any position other than neutral or park, valves in the gearbox operate the brake bands and clutches so that the epicyclic train is able to find a suitable ratio, according to engine load, to the final drive unit.

With the automatic gearbox removed, its external appearance gives the impression of being simple – a nice compact unit that might lead the unwary into thinking that an overhaul is easy. This is far from the case. Upon the launch of the automatic Transporter,

the American journal *PV4* was surprisingly complimentary about it, commenting: 'The performance figures of the automatic van rival those of the stick shift Bus... it's a good transmission. There seems to be little power loss through the 'box. The shift is positive and snappy. The first gear ratio is low enough to move away from the stoplights at a brisk pace. Coupled with the automatic is a rear axle ratio change. At first glance this would indicate lower cruising rpm for the automatic, probably resulting in the engine lugging at highway speed. However, at 70mph both vehicles are turning about the same rpm. This is because the top gear in the automatic is 1:1 or straight through whereas top gear in the 4-speed manual is actually an overdrive ratio of 0.82:1.'

The gearbox ratios for automatic Transporters were the same in the 1700 and 1800 versions and are as follows: first, 2.65:1; second, 1.59:1; third, 1:1; reverse, 1.80:1. The final drive ratio, however, differs between the two at 4.45:1 (1700) or 4.86:1 (1800). One particularly significant difference between manuals and automatics is the length of the driveshafts; the manual's are both 476mm (18.7in) whereas the automatic's are asymmetric at 456mm (17.9in) left and 504mm (19.8in) right.

With the introduction of the 2-litre Transporter, the clutch plate was increased to 228mm (8.98in) diameter and automatics had altered gearbox ratios, as follows: first, 2.55:1; second, 1.45:1; third, 1:1; reverse, 2.46:1. From August 1975 there were improvements to the automatic gearbox, which included mechanical 'kickdown' instead of electrical operation, separate forward and reverse planetary gears, discs instead of bands for first and reverse braking, and a mechanical linkage instead of a vacuum system for signalling engine speed.

From November 1976 the gearchange rod on manual transmissions was supported by three bushes; for many years the linkage rod between the base of the lever and the gearbox was prone to rattling, particularly on high mileage examples, and this modification went a long way to curing the problem.

WHEELS & TYRES

With the Beetle the 4½J wheels changed from the familiar five-stud pattern to a four-stud fixing when the 1500 was launched in August 1966, but the Transporter continued with a five-stud pattern through to the end of production in 1979. This was a 'belt-and-braces' decision because of the Transporter's additional weight and load-carrying capacity. The wheels were 5J×14in items made of steel and to the same design as the Split-screen's until August 1970, when the size increased to 5½J×14 and, instead of there being four narrow slots between rim and centre, there was a series of round holes punctured in the outside of the centre section. This change coincided with the introduction of front disc brakes, and at the same

time the arrangement of the five studs changed from 'wide' to 'narrow'.

The wheels continued to be painted white until August 1970, when the finish changed to silver. While all Beetles from 1965 were fitted with flat hubcaps instead of the earlier domed type, Transporters retained the latter until August 1970, when they too acquired the rather plain, flat variety. As before, hubcaps were painted light grey, except on Microbuses on which they were chromed. Many owners of other vehicles in the range also fitted chromed hubcaps out of choice.

For the 1972 model year, the tubeless crossply tyres that had been fitted from 1967 as standard – except on the Microbus L which had 185×14 radials from the beginning of production – were at last changed for radials (except on 1600 models), mostly supplied by Continental. Unusually, they were fitted with inner tubes, another belt-and-braces decision. In reality most owners sensibly switched to radials after their first set of crossplies wore out, a happy event which rarely took very long.

Some journalists considered that the change to radials was a courageous move, because the extra grip might put undue strain on the suspension and hub assemblies. This was far from the truth; Volkswagen had done its homework properly and the decision turned out to be correct. Another big bonus with radials was that suddenly the vehicle could stop in a straight line as well as virtually any contemporary saloon, and without any of the wheel-locking histrionics that so many owners had experienced with

Unlike contemporary Beetles, which had flat hubcaps and four-stud 15in wheels, the Transporter continued with domed hubcaps and five-stud 14in wheels. Both of these wheels (top row) have optional features: chromed embellishers (left) and whitewall tyres (right). After introduction of front disc brakes in August 1970, wheel rims contained ventilation holes and flatter hubcaps were fitted. Chromed trims with similar apertures were available from dealers' showrooms.

crossplies. A Transporter on crossplies? No thanks. Perish the thought.

Whitewall tyres were extra-cost options on the Microbus L, and they proved to be considerably more popular in North America than anywhere else.

SUSPENSION

Despite starting with a fresh sheet of paper for the overall design of the Bay-window model, the famous independent torsion bar system was retained front and rear. It is a simple layout, inherently robust, and remains unsurpassed to this day for reliability and longevity. Journalists and customers alike sang the praises of this part of the Transporter for years.

The front suspension is much the same as the Beetle's, except that the Transporter's was beefed up for obvious reasons. The torsion bars are contained within two transverse tubes, one above the other, and are larger than the ones fitted to Splitties. The torsion bars are made up of nine individual torsion leaves clamped together one on top of another. At the centre of each bar the leaves are clamped to the torsion tubes. The outer ends of the bars pivot on needle roller bearings and plain bushes, and are connected to the parallel trailing arms on each side with bolts. The torsion leaves require fresh lubricant every 6000 miles, the three nipples being located in the centre and on the outer ends of the torsion tubes.

Hydraulic shock absorbers were supplied by Boge or Fichtel & Sachs, and are vertically located between the top turrets of the suspension uprights and to the lower trailing arm flange. A single bolt is used to secure them at either end. Unlike the Beetle, whose front axle beam is bolted directly to the chassis frame-head, the Transporter's is bolted to the main longitudinal legs of the chassis frame.

As before an anti-roll bar is fitted and connected to rubber-damped clips to the two lower trailing arms. Steering knuckles are supported on maintenance-free upper and lower ball joints by the torsion arms.

At the rear the torsion bars are also housed in a transverse tube situated in front of the gearbox and stretching across the width of the chassis. The inner ends of the bars – and there is only one solid torsion bar on each side – are locked together at the centre by a splined collar. The outer ends of the torsion bars are splined to the longitudinal trailing arms, but differ from the Split-screen's arrangement in having diagonal arms attached on their inner ends to the chassis frame by a bolt – on which it pivots – that passes through a rubber bush. On its outer end the arm is bolted to the trailing arm. The hub and bearing is attached to the outer ends of the trailing arms by bolts, and the shock absorbers are bolted to the wheel hub at the bottom and to the bodywork at the top.

Severe up and down suspension movement is kept in check by meaty rubber buffers, attached to the underframe, that come into contact with a steel cup on the trailing arms. As the driveshafts are fitted with constant velocity joints, each of the rear wheels has the inherent ability to travel in a vertical plane, unlike the Split-window's swinging-axle system in which the wheels are only able to move partially through the

While other manufacturers were increasingly turning to MacPherson strut suspension, Transporter continued with well-proven Porsche-designed torsion bar system with twin parallel trailing arms. These are views of front end, where braking changed from drums (left) to discs (right) in August 1970. Note different configuration of five-stud wheel fixings and central ribbing on drum brake.

radius of a circle. In theory the revised system was safer but, in practice, the vast majority of Transporter owners would never drive at anything approaching the speed whereby a difference between the two systems would be noticed.

The American publication *Popular Imported Cars* commented in its March 1968 road test: 'The final result of these suspension changes is passenger car like ride and handling that has to be tried to be believed. The road for this vehicle has been almost miraculously smoothed and even hard bumps are easily taken at speed. The handling properties are neutral up to all practical cornering speeds and body lean negligible. Heavy side winds can still be felt, but the resulting vehicle movements are largely self-correcting.'

Part of the reason for an improvement in roadholding over the Split-screen model was the increase in track, which went up to 1426mm (56.1in) at the rear and 1384mm (45.5in) at the front. When disc brakes were introduced in August 1970, the front track was again increased by 2mm. Although the front torsion bars remained at 980mm (38.6in) in length, their fitting angle changed in August 1969 from 56° 30′ to 60° 1′.

At the rear the torsion bars differed in size and strength between Transporters specifically designed to carry freight or passengers. From 1967 the former had 28.1mm diameter bars (increased to 28.9mm in August 1970) and the latter had 26.2mm diameter bars (increased to 26.9mm in August 1970).

STEERING

As the Transporter retained front torsion bar suspension (the 1302 Beetle had MacPherson struts from 1970), the large 12-metre (39ft) turning circle was as inconvenient as ever, but the relatively low gearing, which allowed 2.8 turns from lock to lock, certainly helped when it came to negotiating corners. Parking in tight spaces, though, remained an interesting exercise, especially for owners who never got used to the exact whereabouts of the four corners of the body.

For its first four years of production the Baywindow had the tried, tested and well-proven worm-and-peg steering box, which gave reasonably light, precise steering with just a little play at the wheel to indicate that everything is adjusted properly and in good health. A hydraulic steering damper was fitted as standard, of course, and is bolted at one end to the steering swing lever and at the other to a bracket welded directly to the front axle tube. The fixing bolts at each end are both rubber-bushed.

As on Split-screens, the linkage from the steering box is a necessarily complex affair, as the near-vertical steering column is situated ahead of the front axle. From the steering box, a Pitman (or drop) arm is connected by a ball joint to a drag link which is attached, via a ball joint to a swing lever. The latter is connected directly to the unequal length tie-rods

which, in turn, are connected to the wheels with maintenance-free ball joints.

From August 1972 the faithful worm-and-peg steering box was replaced by a worm-and-roller unit, which works in much the same manner except that a roller instead of a peg is used to engage the worm. The idea behind this change was simply to increase the contact area between the two components and thereby reduce the rate at which they wear out. Not that the earlier type gives up the ghost much before 100,000 miles or so, but the new unit's long-term prospects were certainly improved. As before the steering box was adjustable and filled with SAE 90 oil, which in theory should never need changing.

The steering column tube is attached to the cab floor and to the inner skin of the front panel or facia board. Because the column and tube sit vertically in front of the driver, the possibility of chest injuries occurring as a result of a collision are fairly remote. However, after June 1974 the column was modified, not only to accept revised switchgear, but also to make the bolts holding the column to the facia shear automatically. If in the event of an accident the driver was forced at high speed against the steering wheel, the column would tilt forward to reduce the impact against the driver's body.

BRAKING

Braking is one particular aspect of the Bay-window that proved to be a great improvement over the Split-screen, especially after the introduction of front disc brakes in August 1970.

Until August 1970 drum brakes were fitted to all four wheels and were, of course, hydraulically operated. As before, there were two leading shoes at the front and a leading and a trailing shoe at the rear. Two cylinders were employed in each of the front drums,

Rear suspension continued with transverse torsion bars and trailing arms, but hub reduction gearboxes of Split-screen models no longer featured, and much narrower driveshafts were double-jointed in Porsche fashion to improve roadholding.

Drums were used for rear braking throughout production, but without central ribbing found on front drums. Brake adjustment on pre-August 1970 vehicles, as here, is carried out by inserting a screwdriver in the 'sixth' hole seen on the outer face of the drum.

with just one sufficing in each of the rears. As before the shoes were adjustable by inserting a screwdriver through a hole into a threaded adjuster that is moved by a notched wheel, this hole being in the outer face of the drum until August 1970 and in the back plate after that date.

The drums are 250mm (9.84in) in diameter with a lining width of 55mm (2.17in) at the front and a lining surface area of 568sq cm (88.0sq in). The wheel cylinders are 25.4mm (1.00in) in diameter but, from 1971, the rears were reduced in size to 23.81mm (0.84in). The rear drums are the same diameter as those at the front but with 45mm (1.77in) wide linings. The handbrake is of the mechanical type operating on the rear wheels only, the cables running in a conduit through the centre of the chassis. A handbrake adjuster is fitted under the rubber glove at the base of the handbrake lever.

For safety reasons, a dual-circuit system was implemented from the beginning, and the hydraulic tandem master cylinder fitted in front of the foot pedal is considerably larger than the old single-circuit one it replaced. To ensure instant braking response, the master cylinder piston is fitted with a spring-loaded valve that maintains a certain amount of pressure in the brake pipes at all times but not quite enough to operate the brakes. The bore of the master cylinder is 22.2mm (0.87in). Hydraulic brake fluid is stored in a plastic reservoir attached to the bulkhead below the dashboard in the cab.

From August 1970 the braking system was modified to include ATE discs at the front, some four years after the 1500 Beetle was treated to this most worthwhile change. Each disc brake assembly is bolted to the front suspension assembly and each caliper is attached to the steering knuckle. The discs are protected from water and mud by a back plate, which is also bolted to the steering knuckle. The calipers are

in two pieces and bolted together with six bolts. Two of the six bolts pass through the steering knuckle to secure the caliper housing. Unlike the linings of the earlier drum brakes, the pads are self-adjusting.

The discs are 278.2mm (10.95in) in diameter, 13mm (0.5in) thick and have two 54mm (2.13in) diameter caliper pistons in each assembly. Each of the four pads when new was 10mm thick, Volkswagen recommending a minimum thickness of 2mm. In practice, pads were usually changed a week or two after the vehicle's owner could hear them scraping on the discs, which is not to be recommended. The overall pad surface area is 152sq cm (23.56sq in). At the same time the rear drums were made detachable from the hubs, and the linings were increased in width to 55mm (2.17in), giving an overall lining surface area of 550sq cm (84.08sq in). The new master cylinder also had a smaller bore of 20.64mm (0.81in).

All disc brake models were fitted with a hydraulic pressure-regulating valve in the rear circuit that changed the braking pressure to the rear wheels to suit load conditions under braking and deceleration. This was installed because the discs at the front were much more powerful than the rear drums and, without a regulator, the nose of the vehicle would have dipped severely under braking. The regulator itself is nothing more than a ball and two spring-loaded pistons which act to reduce hydraulic pressure. A mechanical brake servo was also fitted when the 1700 model was introduced, and works under the pressure difference between the vacuum in the inlet manifold and atmospheric pressure.

From August 1971, the master cylinder was fitted with two switches instead of one as previously. As before one worked the brake lights, but the other actuated a warning light on the dashboard to indicate when the pressure in the two braking circuits was equalised. If the braking system is working properly this warning light goes out after the ignition switch is actuated, but stays on if there is a fault such as a leak in the system. Naturally, it may also come on when the vehicle is driven and must not be ignored: during the 1950s and '60s, a good many Volkswagen owners usually attributed an illuminated warning light (of any kind) to a faulty electrical switch, and in most cases they were correct, but no such assumptions should be made with the brake warning light.

From September 1975, the trusty ATE front disc calipers were swapped for similar ones from Girling and fitted with 14mm (0.55in) thick pads. At the same time the fluid header tank was placed below the driver's seat and had a small window in front of it to show the correct fluid level.

The disc brake models from 1970 were undoubtedly far superior, their stopping ability rivalling that of most contemporary saloon cars. Too much pressure on the brake pedal at high speeds can make the front wheels lock up, but this is a normal trait of most rear-engined vehicles.

SPECIAL TRANSPORTERS

Volkswagen produced an ambulance version, designated Type 27, from 3 December 1951, although a similar conversion had been available since November 1950 supplied by Miesen in Bonn. The Type 27 was based on the Kombi, but differed at the start in that it had a small engine lid and a separate large tailgate (hinged at the bottom) for easier access to the interior. All other Transporters had to wait until March 1955 for the 'barndoor' to be replaced by this separate tailgate (but hinged at the top) and small engine lid.

Jointly developed by the German ambulance service and Volkswagen, this vehicle had stronger torsion-bar springing, two modern stretchers positioned side by side (rather than one on top of the other) to give patients more headroom, two 'casualty' chairs (one of them portable) and a folding seat. A bottom-hinged folding plate over the width of the rear tailgate ensured that bus stretchers could be guided into the 'passenger' compartment easily. When this plate was folded upwards, it stood vertically at the rear of each stretcher. A buzzer allowed patients to keep in contact with the driver, and roller blinds were

provided for the windows. An electrically-operated fresh air ventilator was fitted to the centre of the roof, and a large flashing blue light to the front.

The interior equipment was strictly for medicinal use only, with a cabinet for medicines and bandages, and special fittings for carrying blood plasma. A glass partition was fitted between cab and passenger area, there was a foot-operated retracting step below the side doors, and an emergency trailer could also be supplied. Additional equipment was usually provided by the hospitals to which these vehicles were sold.

Volkswagen ambulances were available in most foreign markets officially, but were only rarely seen outside Germany because the majority of health authorities in foreign markets had a policy of buying home-grown vehicles. Apart from this, the Volkswagen's engine, being positioned at the rear, was hardly made for a conveniently low loading height. Front-engined vehicles by comparison had a back door that opened just above ground height, which was more convenient for getting patients in and out.

Volkswagen also supplied a fire tender, Type 21F based on the regular Panelvan, specially equipped to

Mainly sold in the German market, Ambulance version was based on Kombi and fitted with a variety of special equipment. This one was built on 17 January 1957 and bears chassis number 224 501.

Hinged at the bottom and with the handle at the top, Split-screen Ambulance's windowless tailgate acts as stretcher support when putting a patient on board. Interior medical equipment differed from hospital to hospital, but Ambulance basics included chairs for patients and medical staff, a stretcher, first aid kit and storage cupboards.

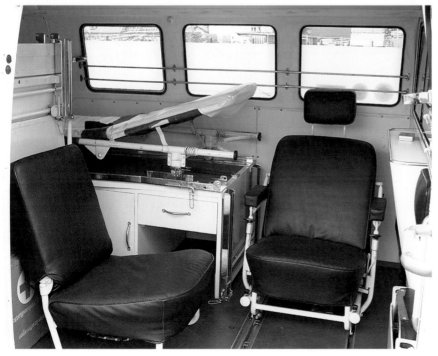

meet the needs of the German fire-fighting service with dry-powder fire extinguishing equipment. And the German army was supplied with vehicles specially converted for military use with attachments for firearms in the cab, a zipped map pocket in the cab's headlining, canvas 'blackout' covers for the window glass and exterior lamps, a comprehensive first-aid kit and other army-related equipment.

In addition, there was a host of Transporters converted for use by officially sanctioned special coachbuilders. The vast majority were for use in Germany by public service utilities, although some were for private trade use as well.

Versions of the Panelvan included a mobile workshop, display van with a folding metal side awning, refrigerator van with a dry-ice blower, a butcher's van with special fittings for hanging meat, a cinema and loudspeaker van, and one with hardboard interior panelling. In addition, there was a version with aluminium interior panelling to insulate the cargo area against extremes of heat and cold.

Pick-up versions included examples with a hydraulic service tower, hydraulic tipping gear, a box

body, jinker, swivelling extension ladder, a box-type jinker, or a load bed without folding flaps. A hearse offered by Frickinger took the form of a Double-cab Pick-up with suitable bodywork constructed above and behind the load bed.

Kombis were supplied to the police force with radar and accident equipment, and to other services kitted out with all sorts of weird and wonderful gadgetry. There was a mobile office, hardwood interior panelling, an expedition Kombi, a delivery van with special shelving and one fitted with water purifying equipment. Microbuses were converted into mobile banks, radar detection vans supplied without seats, school buses, cable repair vans and control vehicles for firefighting authorities – and there was even one with a special sliding glass partition between the cab and passenger area. This glass partition was also fitted to Luxury Microbuses, many of which also had a foot-operated retracting step below the side doors.

A minority of Volkswagen enthusiasts have taken great interest in these special vehicles – all of which continued to the end of Bay-window production – in recent times, and some have gone to the considerable trouble of restoring them to their original condition. Needless to say they are great crowd-pullers at

Bright red fire tender was particularly useful, as it was smaller and faster than traditional appliances. This April 1967 example has added interest for its sliding side door, an optional feature on Split-screen models from March 1963. Seen within are original fire pump using air-cooled VW engine, searchlight, water hose attachments and storage compartments.

Double-cab Pick-up was a firm favourite with German armed forces, because of its ability to carry vast quantities of equipment and up to six personnel. Owned by Mark Anderson, this example, chassis number 266 212 5258 built in May 1976, has 'black-out' coverings in place over windows, headlamps and mirrors.

First aid equipment and gun-holder brackets on floor and dashboard were included in military version's special equipment. Distributor and coil were also specially adapted to cope with deep water.

Volkswagen meetings because of their rarity and the important role they played in Germany's post-war social history.

For the 1978 model year Volkswagen offered a special of its own in the form of the Luxury Microbus painted in smart metallic silver. A special edition Beetle painted the same colour appeared at the same time. Also in 1978, the factory made five four-wheel drive versions of the Bay-window Transporter but, regrettably, this did not get beyond prototype stage. It was perceived by management that the 'leisure market' was not strong enough to warrant such a model at the time.

DATA SECTION

OPTIONS & ACCESSORIES

Study the shape and size of the Transporter for a couple of hours, and it will soon become apparent that it leaves itself wide open to the 'after-market' accessory specialists. Almost from its inception, independent manufacturers queued up to provide Transporter owners with bits and pieces to enhance their vehicles. Volkswagen, who were far too busy actually manufacturing vehicles, were slow to cash in on such trivia and ultimately never caught up with the independents, whose ingenuity in creating accessories was seemingly never-ending.

In the early days Volkswagen provided only a few extra-cost options and accessories, generally limited to a pair of rear mudflaps – large black rubber items with the Wolfsburg crest or V-over-W emblem – and a radio set and aerial. Most radios supplied through dealerships were made by Blaupunkt, but Telefunken and Becker were also common before 1955. Blaupunkt radios, in particular, are wonderfully simple and seem to last forever, and it did not seem to matter to most owners that they are almost inaudible when the engine revs rise above 2500rpm.

The most important and prolific accessories supplier throughout the 1950s and '60s was Karl Meier, an ex-Volkswagen employee who founded his company, Kamei, in 1949. Meier began by retrimming Beetles in bright colours before going on to manufacture a whole host of Beetle accessories, many of which were suitable for the Transporter. There were plastic foot rests for the clutch foot, seat covers, chromed gear lever extensions, a small wastepaper basket for mounting on the dashboard, armrests and head restraints.

The famous alloy chin spoiler that Meier made for the Beetle and exhibited at the 1953 Geneva Motor Show was never intended initially for the Transporter. In fact it never caught on with the Beetle either, which is why Kamei dropped the idea until the 1970s, when the company marketed a plastic aerofoil that fitted just below the front bumper. These were popular with Beetle owners because they arguably improved the frontal appearance, and more importantly helped with stability in cross-winds, but the occasional Bay-window owner also fitted a Kamei plastic spoiler.

Additional dashboard instruments were always popular, and these were also supplied by other independent specialists. In Britain they included Speedwell, of which the famous racing driver Graham Hill was a director. The company made tachometers, oil temperature gauges, ammeters and numerous other 'goodies', including a rear anti-roll bar. A number of companies in Germany provided fuel gauges until Volkswagen fitted one as standard. In addition there was an anti-theft device for locking the gear lever into position, while a combined ignition/starter/steering lock for the column was available long before Volkswagen fitted one as standard.

Bodywork embellishments were supplied by dozens of manufacturers. These included full-width exterior sun visors, roof racks (commonly supplied by Westfalia), chrome or plastic grilles for the air intake louvres (and fresh-air intake on the front panel of Bay-window models), and the famous 'eyelids' that fitted over the headlamps. The latter were

Of all the extras available for Splitties, opening 'Safari' windows are the most perennially sought.

outlawed in Germany during the 1960s because they were thought to pose a potential safety hazard to pedestrians. Despite this, and the fact that they have a detrimental effect on aerodynamic drag, they appear to be popular once again.

Hella and Bosch both supplied spot and fog lamps from the early days of Volkswagen production, and Transporter and Beetle owners snapped them up by the bucketload on account of the poor six-volt headlamps. One interesting accessory available after 1955 – but for the German market only – was a small pod that screwed to the engine lid above the number plate; it contains the illumination bulb and is similar in shape to those fitted to post-1963 Beetles. This is rare today and of historical interest, but of doubtful aesthetic or practical value.

Desirable on Split-screens, particularly in hot countries, were the 'Safari' opening windscreens. The two halves of the screen were hinged at the top, each opened by two simple catches – an excellent means of getting an instant stream of fresh air into the cab. Naturally, these never featured on the Bay-window model with the large single-piece windscreen.

Throughout the 1970s, Volkswagen began to offer more in the way of extra-cost options and accessories, but they varied markedly from country to country. Dealers typically supplied towbars, spot and fog lamps, mudflaps, steel sliding sunroofs, electrically-heated rear windows (but not on all models), inertia reel seat belts, radios, halogen headlamps and car care products.

Today, many accessories, such as dashboard flower vases, have become much sought-after by collectors everywhere. Early Kamei products are particularly rare, and therefore expensive, but the decision to fit all the bits and pieces must ultimately lie with personal preference.

An excess of electrical equipment puts a massive strain on the battery, and the rest just add weight to what is already a heavy vehicle. The 'bonnet' bibs that have become popular of late will certainly protect the front panel from stone chippings, but these tend to trap moisture and cause corrosion if left in place for a long time. The same applies to the alloy finger plates that fit behind the door handles.

Optional extras are defined by Volkswagen 'M' numbers and, when factory-fitted, itemised on the 'M number plate'. Little official documentation exists, but research by Michael Steinke (Bulli-Archiv, Germany) and Steve Saunders (Split-Screen Van Club, UK) has resulted in the following lists of 'M' numbers for Split-screen and Bay-window models.

SPLIT-SCREEN M NUMBERS

M 010 Dust filters for passenger compartment
M 013 Hardboard trim for load area and two benches
M 015 Windscreen washers
M 016 Pick-up with Double-cab (this became a model in its own right from June 1964)
M 017 Rear brake and tail lights combined
M 019 With 200-watt dynamo
M 020 Speedometer in miles per hour
M 024 Sealed beam headlights and red tail lights (US)
M 025 US-spec bumpers and six pop-out windows
M 026 Activated charcoal exhaust filter (US, Canada & Japan)
M 028 Ambulance without stretchers
M 029 Towing hooks front and rear
M 030 Coupled headlight flasher and number plate lamp (Austria)

M 031 Underside primered, not painted
M 032 Locking fuel filler cover
M 033 Additional rear flashing indicators, to chassis 802 985 (Italy and Australia)
M 034 Side flashing indicators & modified handbrake
M 035 Side marker lights
M 036 Parking light warning lamp, side flashing indicators and modified handbrake lever (Italy)
M 037 Without hazard warning lights (Italy)
M 040 Speedometer with fuel gauge (?)
M 043 Complies with Swiss market regulations
M 046 Side flashing indicators (Denmark)
M 047 Two reversing lights
M 051 Prepared for second dynamo
M 052 Tailgate without window (to March 1955)
M 053 Tailgate with window (to March 1955)
M 054 Full-width dashboard (standard from March 1955)
M 055 Twin fans in roof ventilator (not the same as M 121)
M 056 Steering/ignition lock
M 057 Split front seats ('walk-through')
M 059 Thermostatic carburettor pre-heat control
M 060 Eberspächer stationary heater for Pick-up and Ambulance (to March 1955)
M 062 Passenger side exterior mirror
M 064 Pick-up supplied without side and tail flaps
M 065 Axle weight limit plate
M 066 Rubber flooring for load area
M 069 As M 013 but for Kombi with sliding door on left
M 070 Canvas tilt for Pick-up
M 071 Second locker bed door for Pick-up
M 072 Vinyl headlining (standard from October 1964)
M 074 Mud flaps, rear only
M 075 Mud flaps
M 077 Underseal – Double-cab Pick-up
M 078 Underseal – Pick-up
M 080 Walk-through cab (Panelvan and Kombi, LHD)
M 081 Walk-through cab (Microbus and Samba, LHD)
M 082 Walk-through cab (?)
M 089 Laminated windscreen (depends on type)
M 090 Laminated windscreen (depends on type)
M 091 Whitewall tyres
M 092 Gear ratios for mountainous regions
M 093 Fresh air vent above split screen (to March 1955)
M 094 Locking engine lid
M 095 Radio – Wolfsburg model
M 096 Radio – Braunschweig model
M 097 Radio – Emden model
M 099 M & S Tyres (tubeless)
M 100 Supplied without front VW badge
M 101 M & S tyres for Type 21F (fire tender)
M 102 Heated rear window
M 103 Heavy-duty shock absorbers (?)
M 105 Harder gearbox mountings (?)
M 106 Heavy-duty shock absorbers
M 107 Crash bars (?)
M 108 Camping equipment (Westfalia SO42)
M 113 'Safari' windscreens
M 114 Six opening side windows

Rare but not that desirable owing to the fire risk it brings: Eberspächer stationary petrol heater.

Wheel perimeter trims were available as extra-cost options on most, but not all, models throughout Splittie and Bay eras.

M 115 Low loader (special Pick-up type)
M 116 Without vents in load area (Panelvan)
M 118 Pick-up supplied without side and tail flaps
M 119 Eberspächer stationary heater (except Ambulance)
M 121 With fresh air blower in roof peak
M 123 Special suppression equipment
M 124 Yellow headlight bulbs (for France)
M 127 Tailgate without window
M 129 34bhp engine
M 130 Samba without sliding roof and skylight windows
M 132 'Safari' windscreens with laminated glass
M 137 Type 23F: Kombi equipped as fire personnel carrier
M 139 Sealed-beam headlamps and red rear lenses
M 140 Fire truck preparation (Type 21F)
M 141 With heating in load area
M 142 Laminated glass for side windows (Kombi/Microbus)
M 143 Laminated glass for side windows (Samba)
M 144 Laminated glass for side windows (Ambulance)
M 145 Safety lock for sliding door models
M 146 As M 013 but for seven-seater
M 150 Full Ambulance equipment
M 151 Eberspächer stationary heater (Ambulance)
M 152 Tailgate panel with extension (Ambulance)
M 155 Air cleaner with additional cyclone filter
M 156 Larger air cleaner (or second mirror?)
M 157 Exhaust emissions equipment
M 160 With blue light and siren
M 161 Sliding door (Panelvan – one side)
M 162 Sliding door (Panelvan – both sides)
M 163 Sliding door (Microbus)
M 164 Flashing front indicators (1950s)
M 164 Sliding door for Samba (1960s)
M 168 88Ah battery (six-volt)
M 169 Sliding door (Kombi)
M 171 Tyres with high load rating
M 172 Visible location of brake fluid reservoir
M 173 Engine prepared for arctic climates
M 175 'American' bumpers (except Pick-ups)
M 176 'American' bumpers (Pick-ups)
M 177 Rear seat only (no central bench, depending on type)
M 178 Rev limiter for 1200cc engine
M 180 Rear seat only (no central bench, depending on type)
M 181 Chrome hubcaps
M 183 Walk-through cab (Panelvan/Kombi, RHD)
M 184 Walk-through cab (Microbus/Samba, RHD)
M 187 Asymmetrical headlamps, RHD (depending on type)
M 188 Asymmetrical headlamps, RHD (depending on type)
M 191 Protective plates below chassis
M 192 Basic equipment for Camper
M 193 Semaphore indicators in red
M 194 Larger door mirrors
M 196 Asymmetrical headlamps, RHD (depending on type)
M 199 Driver's seat swivel
M 200 Pick-up with extended platform
M 201 Pick-up with extended wooden platform
M 203 Eberspächer stationary heater (Double-cab Pick-up)
M 207 Tilt and bows (Double-cab Pick-up)

M 208 Towing equipment
M 211 Seating for nine persons, sliding doors both sides
M 215 1 ton payload and 1500cc engine (standard from October 1964)
M 216 1500cc engine (standard from October 1964)
M 220 Limited slip differential
M 221 High-roof van with sales flap
M 222 High-roof delivery van
M 223 Low loader without guide rails (Westfalia Pick-up)
M 224 Low loader with guide rails (Westfalia Pick-up)
M 240 Low compression engine for low-octane fuels (engine code 'L')
M 303 Complies with Italian regulations
M 361 Package: M 168, M 181, M 192 and M 199
M 367 Package: M 361, M 020, M 024, M 090, M 142 and M 175
M 369 Package = M 361, M 020, M 024, M 113, M 142, M 132 and M 175
M 362 Prepared for US market
M 396 Complies with UK market regulations
M 430 For US market, including dual-circuit brakes
M 502 Patterned hardboard side panelling
M 503 Patterned hardboard roof panelling
M 504 Patterned hardboard panelling, not walk-through
M 505 Patterned hardboard panelling, walk-through
M 510 Panelvan hardboard partition, with window
M 513 Protective skids for area below gearbox
M 515 Articulated unit
M 520 Sliding doors left and right
M 525 Seat belts (US)
M 527 Large rear tailgate
M 529 Cab partition sliding window
M 530 Automatic step for loading doors
M 531 Harder springing for rear
M 535 Tachograph
M 539 Automatic step
M 543 Supplied without seating in load area (Types 22 & 24)
M 546 Flashing indicators on roof at rear
M 616 Reversing light
M 620 12-volt electrical system (standard from August 1966)
M 621 Hazard warning lights
M 623 Fully suppressed 12-volt system
M 718 Red Cross lighting
M 729 Michelin X radial tyres (tubeless)

BAY-WINDOW M NUMBERS
M 010 Additional dust proofing for engine compartment (models 211-274)
M 013 Front and rear bench seats in passenger compartment and interior trim panels (models 231, 235)
M 019 Without headlamp flasher to chassis number 219 300 000 (models 211-274)
M 020 Speedometer reading in miles per hour (models 211-274)
M 024 Sealed beam headlamps to chassis number 219 300 000 (models 211-268); export (not for US and Canada)
M 024 Sealed beam headlamps, side repeater flashers and reversing lamp from chassis number 210 2000 001 (models 211-268); export (not for US and Canada)
M 026 Active carbon canister for emission control (models 211-274); California only
M 029 Front and rear towing hooks to chassis number 211 2300 000 (models 211-268)
M 030 Headlamp flasher and simultaneous number plate illumination, LHD (models 211-271), Austria only
M 032 Locking petrol filler cap to chassis number 211 2300 000 (models 211-274)
M 034 Side repeater flashers and modified handbrake lever (models 211-274), Italy only
M 037 Without hazard warning flashers (models 211-274), France and Italy only
M 046 Side repeater flashers (LHD), and from chassis number 219 060 789 to 219 300 000 wit interior rear view mirror (models 211-271), Denmark only
M 047 Reversing lamp to chassis number 211 2300 000 (models 211-268)
M 050 Warning lamp for dual-circuit braking system (models 211-274)
M 053 Cloth instead of vinyl upholstery (models 221-228, 241, 244)
M 054 Locking glovebox (models 221-228, 241, 244)
M 055 Steering lock to chassis number 219 300 000 (models 211-274)

M 062 Exterior rear view mirror, right-hand side, convex, (LHD); interior rear view mirror with shorter stem to chassis number 219 300 000 (models 211-271), Sweden only
M 062 Right-hand sun visor without mirror from chassis number 211 2000 001 (models 221-225, 241), Sweden only
M 070 Tarpaulin tilt for Pick-up (models 261, 264)
M 071 Second dropside panel to Pick-up bed (models 261, 264)
M 074 Rear mudflap (models 211-268)
M 089 Laminated glass windscreen (models 211-268)
M 092 Low final drive for mountain areas (models 211-274)
M 102 Heated rear window (models 211-268)
M 103 Heavy-duty shock absorbers for poor roads (models 211-274)
M 119 Eberspächer stationary heating system (models 211-244)
M 121 Fresh-air ventilation with electric fan (models 211-274)
M 123 Radio interference suppression equipment (models 211-274), export only
M 124 Yellow headlamps and safety framed rear view mirror (models 211-274), France only
M 127 Rear hatch without window (models 211-235)
M 130 Without steel sunroof (models 241, 244)
M 140 Fully equipped fire engine (models 231, 235)
M 145 Safety locks for sliding door and rear hatch (models 211, 215)
M 146 Two-passenger front bench seat and rear bench seat in passenger compartment and interior trim panels (models 231, 235)
M 150 Ambulance to specification DIN 75 080 (model 271)
M 151 Eberspächer stationary heating system (models 271, 274)
M 155 Filter system with dual air filters (models 211-274), export only
M 156 Large-capacity oil bath air filter (models 211-274)
M 157 Exhaust emission control system, from engine number B 5 000 000 to B 5 230 000 and from engine number AE 0 000 001 to AE 0 529 815 (models 211-274), US only
M 160 Beacon and warning siren (models 271, 274)
M 187 Headlights for driving on the left (models 211-274)
M 194 Exterior mirrors, left and right (convex) (models 211-268)

Alloy finger plates behind door handles are more popular than ever these days, but tend to trap moisture and cause corrosion. Styles for the two types of Split-screen cab handle are seen.

M 201 High-capacity wooden load bed for Pick-up (models 261, 264)
M 203 Eberspächer stationary heating system (models 265, 268)
M 207 Tarpaulin tilt for Double-cab Pick-up (models 265, 268)
M 208 Vehicles with trailer (models 211-274)
M 220 Limited-slip differential (models 211-274)
M 221 Opening windows in passenger compartment from chassis number 212 2000 001 (models 211, 215, 231, 235, 261, 265)
M 222 Fixed windows in passenger compartment instead of opening windows, to chassis number 211 2300 001 (models 231, 235)
M 240 Engine with concave top pistons (low compression) for low-octane petrol (models 211-274)
M 248 Ignition lock without steering lock from chassis number 210 2000 001 (models 211-274)
M 251 1.7 litre engine with 66bhp instead of 1.6 litre engine with 50bhp (models 211-241, 271) US only
M 252 1.3 litre engine with 44bhp instead of 1.6 litre engine with 50bhp (models 211-274), Italy only
M 258 High seatbacks (headrests) to driving seat and front passenger seat (models 211-274)
M 500 Full-width division behind driving cabin with two-passenger front passenger seat (models 211-244)
M 501 Two-passenger front passenger seat (models 211-244)
M 502 Interior side panels in hardboard (models 211, 231)
M 503 Interior roof trim panel in hardboard (models 211-216, 231, 234)
M 504 Fresh-air ventilation in load compartment (models 211-216, 231-235, 265, 268)
M 506 Brake servo (LHD) and dual-circuit braking system (models 211-271)
M 507 Quarterlight in driving cab doors (models 211-235, 261-274)
M 508 Opening windows in passenger compartment opposite sliding door, to chassis number 211 2300 000 (models 221-244)
M 508 Opening windows in sliding door and all windows on the opposite side, from chassis number 212 2000 001 (models 221-244)
M 508 Opening windows in passenger compartment door and to side window opposite, from chassis number 212 2000 001 (Double-Cab Pick-up) (models 265-268)
M 509 Air inlet with dust screen, larger oil bath air cleaner and additional engine dust proofing (models 261-268)
M 510 Upper division between cabin and load compartment, only for vehicles fitted with M 500 (models 211-216)
M 511 Padded fascia, LHD only (models 211-271)
M 513 Protective runners for gearbox cover (models 211-274)
M 514 Recirculated air heating (models 211-244, 271, 274)

Two nice features in a 1956 Panelvan: optional Blaupunkt radio (above) and rare accessory clock (below) in centre of steering wheel.

A pod to enclose number plate light – to stop it shining at drivers behind – is rare post-1955 accessory. Specially designed for the Transporter, it was made by Volkswagen and bears a factory part number.

M 515 High-roof Panelvan with higher sliding door (model 211)
M 516 Plastic roof for High-roof Panelvan (models 211, 214)
M 518 Motor caravan with adjustable roof (models 231, 234)
M 519 Ventilation slots (models 211, 214)
M 520 Sliding door on left and right (models 221-244)
M 521 Additional chrome package and sun visor with mirror to chassis number 219 300 000; from chassis number 210 2000 001 without sun visor with mirror (models 221-228)
M 524 Sealed beam headlamps, dual-circuit brakes, reversing lamp and side marker lamps (LHD) from chassis number 219 000 001 without hazard warning flashers, from chassis number 210 2000 001 with audible warning for ignition lock (models 211-265), US and Canada. From chassis number 212 2000 001 (models 211-241), US and Canada
M 525 Seat belts (models 211-265), US and Canada
M 527 Exhaust emission control (only in combination with M 156/M 240), from engine number C 0 000 001 to C 0 100 000 (models 211-274), Japan only
M 527 Exhaust emission control, from engine number AD 0 000 001 (models 211-274), Japan and Sweden only
M 528 Exterior rear view mirror, right-hand side, convex, LHD (models 211-265)
M 529 Sliding window to division behind cab, only for vehicles fitted with M 500 (models 221-244)
M 530 Automatic step board (models 211-244)
M 531 Heavy-duty rear suspension torsion bars (models 221-228, 241, 244)
M 533 Alarm system (models 221, 225, 244)
M 535 Tachograph (models 211-274)
M 537 Transistor light instead of ceiling light (models 221-228, 241, 244)
M 601 Special equipment package consisting of M 47 (reversing lamp), M 102 (heated rear window), hazard warning flashers, dual circuit brakes and padded facia (LHD only), to chassis number 218 220 000 (models 211-268)
M 601 Special equipment package consisting of dual circuit brakes and padded facia, to chassis number 218 220 000 (model 271)
M 602 Special equipment package consisting of: hazard warning flashers, dual circuit brakes and padded facia (LHD only), to chassis number 218 220 000 (models 211-268)
M 652 Interval wipe facility (models 211-274)
M 623? Extended electronic suppression equipment (models 211-274), German army
M 659 Halogen fog lamp (models 211-274)
M 663 High seatback (headrest) to driving seat, RHD only (models 214-274), Japan only

SPLIT-SCREEN (1950-67)

IDENTIFICATION & DATING

CHASSIS PLATE

The chassis plate gives essential information about a vehicle's identity. It is fitted to the engine bulkhead, visible to the right of the engine as you look into the compartment, on vehicles built before late 1963. but thereafter it is found inside the cab on the driver's side of the overhead air box. The number is also stamped into the sheet metal near the battery.

The 'Typ' number is the basic model code: 21 (Panelvan), 22 (Microbus), 23 (Kombi), 24 (Microbus de luxe), 25 (Microbus de luxe seven-seater), 26 (Pick-up), 27 (Ambulance) and 28 (Microbus seven-seater). The 'Fahrgest. Nr' is the chassis number, from which a vehicle can always be dated to a month and year, sometimes even to a specific day.

Until the end of 1955 chassis numbers were prefixed '20'. The prefix was then dropped, but the remaining six figures continued to run in the same sequence until the end of the 1964 model year (July 1964). The 1,000,000th vehicle was built in September 1962, and the last chassis number in this system was 1 328 871.

For the 1965 model year (starting in August 1964) a new system was adopted, once again with a prefix but this time a more informative one with three digits: the first two digits

give the 'Typ' number, and the third denotes the model year (eg, 246 would be a Microbus de luxe built in the 1966 model year, between August 1965 and July 1966). After this prefix, a new six-figure numbering sequence ran from the beginning of each new model year, starting from 000 001 to coincide with the return to work in August after the factory's summer break.

On all vehicles the chassis number is additionally stamped into the engine mounting plate.

Chassis plate, positioned from late 1963 on ventilation box under cab roof (left). Model type (24 for Microbus de luxe) is accompanied by chassis number (1 276 294). Other information concerns vehicle's maximum gross weight

(Gesamtgew) and maximum axle weights (Achslast) at front (Vorn) and rear (Hinten). The very early type of chassis plate on engine bulkhead (above), in this case from 1951 Microbus, has chassis number and year at top right.

*'M number plate',
normally mounted on cab
wall behind right-hand
front seat from late 1958,
gives fascinating range of
information about
original identity. Seen on
Trevor Mouncey's 1964
Samba, figures on this
plate translate as follows.
Top line: day/month of
manufacture; in this case
6 April. Middle line:
three-figure 'M' numbers
listing factory-fitted
options or features for
specific markets; in this
case 374 (unknown), 025*

*(US-spec bumpers and six
pop-out side windows),
056 (steering lock), 139
(US-spec sealed-beam
headlamps and all-red
tail-light lenses) and 216
(1500 engine). Bottom
line: basic vehicle
identification information;
model code on left (241
is LHD Microbus de
luxe, meaning of 3
unknown), paint/trim
codes in centre (45
Sealing Wax Red paint,
44 Beige-Grey paint, 75
Silver-Beige trim), chassis
number on right.*

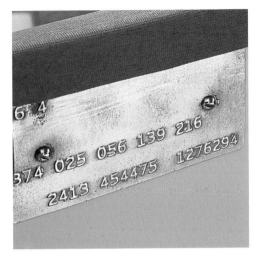

M NUMBER PLATE

This plate, colloquially known as the 'bus plate' and screwed or riveted on the dividing wall behind the right-hand front seat on vehicles built after late 1958, provides more information than the chassis plate, but in an obscure form that has been decoded only in recent years by Split-screen enthusiasts. How to interpret the three rows of figures is explained in the photograph caption, and 'M' number definitions (describing options and market variations) are given on pages 120-122.

There are variations on the April 1964 example shown, the most significant one being the way the date of manufacture is defined. Until 1963 vehicles had five digits (instead of three), additionally giving the year of manufacture:

12 06 9, for instance, would indicate build on 12 June 1959. Our illustrated example, however, appears to represent an anomaly for the 1964 model year alone, since there is no indication of year of manufacture anywhere on the plate – the new 'year-by-year' chassis number system was not introduced until August 1964.

Two other useful points should be made. The post-August 1963 three-digit date code uses numbers 1 to 9 to indicate January to September, but October, November and December are respectively denoted by the letters O, N and D. Body and trim colours (the middle batch of figures in the bottom row) were given in abbreviated letter form on earlier vehicles, but the date of this change is unknown.

MODEL CODES

Panelvan

211	Loading doors right (LHD)
213	Loading doors left (LHD)
214	Loading doors left (RHD)
215	Loading doors both sides (LHD)
216	Loading doors both sides (RHD)

Microbus (nine-seater)

221	Loading doors right (LHD)
223	Loading doors left (LHD)
224	Loading doors left (RHD)
225	Loading doors right, sunroof (LHD)
228	Loading doors left, sunroof (RHD)

Kombi

231	Loading doors right (LHD)
233	Loading doors left (LHD)
234	Loading doors left (RHD)
235	Loading doors right, sunroof (LHD)
237	Loading doors left, sunroof (LHD)
238	Loading doors left, sunroof (RHD)

Microbus de luxe (nine-seater)

241	LHD
242	RHD

Microbus de luxe (seven-seater)

251	Walk-through (LHD)

Pick-up

261	Locker lid right (LHD)
263	Locker lid left (LHD)
264	Locker lid left (RHD)
265	Double-cab, loading door right (LHD)
267	Double-cab, loading door left (LHD)
268	Double-cab, loading door left (RHD)

Ambulance

271	Loading doors right (LHD)
273	Loading doors left (LHD)
274	Loading doors left (RHD)

Microbus (seven-seater)

281	Loading doors right, walk-through (LHD)
285	Loading doors right, walk-through plus sunroof (LHD)

PRODUCTION CHANGES

1950
20-00000? (8 Mar)
First production Transporter (Panelvan).
20-000265 (May)
Right-hand tie rod toe-in changed from 2-5mm to 2-3mm.
20-000770 (Jun)
Grease nipple on steering drag link accessible from above.
20-002818 (Sep)
On Panelvan, three short louvres introduced each side to ventilate load area, positioned high at rear.
20-005001 (31 Oct)
Spare wheel moved from vertical position on right-hand side of engine compartment to horizontal position above engine.
20-005534 (11 Nov)
VW roundel no longer fitted to rear panel (in position where rear window later appeared, at 20-012343); applies to all models.

1951
20-008308 (5 Jan)
Suspension spring plate adjustment altered from 5-6 degrees to 4-5 degrees.
20-011868 (10 Apr)
VW emblem on nose changed from aluminium to steel.
20-012232 (Apr)
Dynamo changed from RED 130/6 AL15 to AL16.
20-012343 (20 Apr)
Small rear window introduced for Panelvan, Kombi and Microbus.
20-012511 (7 May)
Bushes for king and link pins provided with lubrication grooves.
20-013908 (1 Jun)
First Microbus de luxe (Samba): sliding roof, four passenger compartment windows each side, four skylight windows each side, wrap-round rear quarter windows ('23-window').
20-015400 (3 Aug)
Lengthened load compartment ventilation louvres on Panelvan.
20-019498 (3 Dec)
First Ambulance version built at Wolfsburg.

1952
20-020829 (22 Jan)
Tool kit no longer includes grease gun.
20-022910 (17 Mar)
Brake fluid reservoir fitted without float.
20-023750 (31 Mar)
Two red reflectors at rear instead of one on left-hand side.
20-027414 (29 May)
One valve spring instead of two as previously.
20-030222 (11 Jul)
External mirror arm mounted to point downwards instead of upwards.
20-030590 (5 Aug)
First Pick-up built.
20-030868 (Aug)
Fuel filler neck diameter reduced from 100mm to 80mm.

1953
20-041712 (2 Jan)
Quarterlight design changed: front-opening piano hinge replaced by swivelling movement on pins top and bottom; handbrake lever lengthened.
20-045109 (Feb)
Horn relocated from side panel to longitudinal member.
20-046799 (Mar)
Front brake drums with reinforced hubs.
20-047102 (Mar)
Synchromesh on second, third and top gears.
20-053960 (Jun)
Modified exhaust manifold with improved sealing for Pick-up truck.
20-054994 (Jun)
Carburettor ball valves made of bronze instead of steel.
20-055710 (Jun)
Cable between battery and starter shortened from 860mm to 780mm.
20-059939 (Aug)
Tapped insert for sparking plugs; tightening torque increased from 4-5mkg to 7-7.5mkg.
20-066116 (11 Nov)
Pick-up receives strengthening pressings, rectangular in shape, for sideflaps (four) and tailgate (three).
20-069409 (21 Dec)
Introduction of 30bhp 1192cc engine. Dynamo increased in

Supplied in a roll-up bag, Split-screen tool kit changed little, but lacked a spare fan belt after August 1954 – cautious owners, however, are never without one.

power from 130 watt to 160 watt. Speedometer calibrated to 100kph instead of 80kph as previously.

1954
20-090138 (Jul)
Filter element omitted from oil filler neck.
20-098586 (Sep)
Bearing bush in torsion arms has four lubrication grooves instead of three.
20-093601 (Aug)
Spare fan belt no longer included in tool kit.
20-095422 (Aug)
Carburettor 28 PCI main jet changed from 122.5 to 117.5 and air correction jet from 200 to 195.

1955
20-117902 (1 Mar)
Cab roof 'peaked' to allow new interior fresh air ventilation arrangement, air collection and distribution box attached to underside of cab roof, 'barn door' engine lid replaced by opening tailgate (with T handle) and smaller engine lid (opened with 'church key'), nine engine cooling louvres

instead of eight, petrol filler moved to exterior and reduced in diameter to 60mm, revised handle with integral lock for side doors, revised tail lamps with thinner bezels and flat lenses (with integral hexagon-pattern reflectors), cut-outs in front bodywork below wiper spindles, spare wheel moved from engine compartment to a well in the cab behind the seats, chassis frame strengthened. Instead of semaphores, US models have flashing indicators. New design of 'full-width' dashboard fitted to all models, larger speedometer, combined ignition/starter, direction indicator switch transferred from top of dashboard to left-hand side of steering column, steering wheel with two spokes instead of three, stronger windscreen wiper motor, revised accelerator pedal. Air correction jet in 28 PCI carburettor changed from 195 to 180, fuel tap seal changed from Thiokol to cork, oil bath air cleaner modified in shape, wheel diameter reduced from 16in to 15in and tyres changed from 5.50x16 to 6.40x15, Fichtel & Sachs STDZ 26x130 shock absorbers instead of Boge T 27x130, steering damper standard, master brake cylinder diameter increased from 19.05mm to 22.20mm, front wheel brake cylinder diameter increased from 22.20mm to 25.50mm, rear wheel brake cylinder diameter increased from 19.05mm to 22.20mm.

20-124852 (Apr)
Inlet manifold fitted with cast alloy jacket.

20-137738 (Aug)
Single chamber exhaust box with twin connecting pipes for pre-heating tubes. Dynamo pulley securing nut reduced in diameter from 36mm to 21mm.

1956
166 278 (Feb)
Shim fitted between hexagonal screw head and eye of steering damper mounting.

171 056 (8 Mar)
First vehicle produced at Hanover plant, but parallel Wolfsburg/Hanover production occurs for several weeks.

185 697 (Jun)
Fuel sender unit with a copper instead of a cork seal.

188 651 (Jun)
Boge TP 27x162 shock absorbers fitted.

205 985 (Oct)
6.40x15 tubeless tyres fitted to an unknown number of vehicles.

1957
117 449 (Jan)
Brake pipes galvanised.

238 470 (Mar)
Magnetic oil drain plug fitted in place of non-magnetic.

248 322 (Apr)
Brake fluid reservoir cap in rubber instead of screw-on.

250 592 (May)
ATE alternative steering supplier, formerly only ZF.

268 311 (Jun)
6-volt 88Ah battery in place of 77Ah item fitted to vehicles exported to Canada and Alaska.

1958
316 357 (Jan)
Emergency light and alarm signal on fire tender controlled by one switch instead of two.

351 736 (May)
Single central brake light deleted (engine lid pressing changed to suit), brake lights now incorporated in larger tail lamps on each side

361 100 (May)
Carburettor venturi made of plastic instead of metal.

368 390 (Jun)
Suppressed rotor and sparking plug connectors.

374 811 (Aug)
Introduction of finger recess behind exterior handle on side loading door; stronger bumpers with longer blades introduced for all non-US markets; sun visor changed from grey fibreboard to padded vinyl on Microbus (Type 22) and Microbus de luxe (Type 24)

385 000 (Sep)
Introduction of more substantial 'US-spec' bumpers (with overriders and 'nudge' bars) as standard for North America, optional in other markets.

397 288 (3 Nov)
First Double-cab Pick-up.

421 020 (Dec)
Pick-up's rear lights 12mm nearer outside of bodywork.

CHASSIS NUMBER DATING

Each chassis number is the last vehicle produced in the given month

1950		Aug	20-095476	**1959**		May	1 125 405
Apr	20-000372	Sep	20-099251	Jan	433 713	Jun	1 139 905
May	20-000671	Oct	20-102992	Feb	443 662	Jul	1 144 302
Jun	20-001300	Nov	20-106736	Mar	453 140	Aug	1 161 763
Jul	20-001751	Dec	20-110603	Apr	465 351	Sep	1 177 674
Aug	20-002897			May	473 664	Oct	1 194 634
Sep	20-004171	**1955**		Jun	484 280	Nov	1 210 790
Oct	20-005622	Jan	20-114525	Jul	490 622	Dec	1 222 500
Nov	20-007037	Feb	20-118226	Aug	500 151		
Dec	20-008112	Mar	20-122491	Sep	511 539	**1964**	
		Apr	20-126350	Oct	523 532	Jan	1 241 702
1951		May	20-130518	Nov	535 079	Feb	1 259 996
Jan	20-009542	Jun	20-135093	Dec	546 843	Mar	1 276 060
Feb	20-010867	Jul	20-137605			Apr	1 294 464
Mar	20-011741	Aug	20-141925	**1960**		May	1 309 452
Apr	20-012519	Sep	20-146689	Jan	566 342	Jun	1 326 422
May	20-013359	Oct	20-151365	Feb	576 537	Jul	1 328 871
Jun	20-014337	Nov	20-155966	Mar	591 665	Aug	215 019 888*
Jul	20-015323	Dec	20-160735	Apr	601 918	Sep	215 036 650
Aug	20-016345			May	615 192	Oct	215 053 460
Sep	20-017286	**1956**		Jun	628 443	Nov	215 068 246
Oct	20-018355	Jan	165 518	Jul	632 584	Dec	215 082 480
Nov	20-019312	Feb	170 083	Aug	646 458		
Dec	20-020112	Mar	174 402	Sep	660 619	**1965**	
		Apr	178 687	Oct	678 772	Jan	215 098 657
1952		May	183 006	Nov	689 879	Feb	215 114 123
Jan	20-021347	Jun	188 568	Dec	710 069	Mar	215 131 697
Feb	20-022408	Jul	191 466			Apr	215 146 424
Mar	20-023870	Aug	197 451	**1961**		May	215 161 145
Apr	20-025719	Sep	203 492	Jan	723 431	Jun	215 175 741
May	20-027676	Oct	210 631	Feb	739 109	Jul	215 176 339
Jun	20-029572	Nov	217 330	Mar	755 274	Aug	216 020 494
Jul	20-030782	Dec	223 216	Apr	769 247	Sep	216 036 844
Aug	20-032823			May	784 276	Oct	216 052 244
Sep	20-035134	**1957**		Jun	802 130	Nov	216 067 992
Oct	20-037647	Jan	230 857	Jul	804 877	Dec	216 083 207
Nov	20-039772	Feb	237 755	Aug	820 741		
Dec	20-041857	Mar	245 131	Sep	835 178	**1966**	
		Apr	252 041	Oct	850 333	Jan	216 098 498
1953		May	260 394	Nov	871 303	Feb	216 113 500
Jan	20-044361	Jun	267 548	Dec	882 314	Mar	216 130 951
Feb	20-046563	Jul	271 675			Apr	216 145 999
Mar	20-049106	Aug	280 675	**1962**		May	216 162 519
Apr	20-051360	Sep	289 447	Jan	896 977	Jun	216 178 999
May	20-053447	Oct	298 823	Feb	910 310	Jul	216 179 668
Jun	20-056087	Nov	307 428	Mar	925 355	Aug	217 020 467
Jul	20-057628	Dec	315 209	Apr	939 155	Sep	217 036 497
Aug	20-059939			May	954 230	Oct	217 051 659
Sep	20-062598	**1958**		Jun	969 408	Nov	217 066 356
Oct	20-065376	Jan	324 344	Jul	978 018	Dec	217 079 889
Nov	20-067819	Feb	332 599	Aug	989 985		
Dec	20-070431	Mar	341 227	Sep	1 004 496	**1967**	
		Apr	349 562	Oct	1 021 182	Jan	217 091 416
1954		May	357 978	Nov	1 036 923	Feb	217 102 476
Jan	20-073148	Jun	366 867	Dec	1 047 967	Mar	217 110 815
Feb	20-076265	Jul	371 275			Apr	217 120 469
Mar	20-079978	Aug	379 407	**1963**		May	217 133 866
Apr	20-083238	Sep	388 976	Jan	1 062 951	Jun	217 145 796
May	20-086613	Oct	398 980	Feb	1 077 443	Jul	217 148 459
Jun	20-090054	Nov	407 282	Mar	1 093 657		
Jul	20-092166	Dec	416 082	Apr	1 109 397		

*From the start of the 1965 model year, the first two digits represent the model type: numbers found are 21 (Panelvan), 22 (Microbus), 23 (Kombi), 24 (Microbus de luxe), 25 (Microbus de luxe seven-seater) 26 (Pick-up), 27 (Ambulance) and 28 (Microbus seven-seater). In this new chassis numbering system the third digit represents the model year.

422 670 (Dec)
Rear lights 12mm nearer outside of bodywork, all models.

1959
422 999 (Jan)
Hub cap puller included in tool kit.
448 177 (Mar)
Reinforcement plate welded to front axle beam between lower tube and torsion arm stop.
449 484 (Mar)
Exhaust box protected with zinc paint instead of black paint.
468 258 (May)
Ignition leads fastened in pairs by rubber holders to the fan housing.
469 448 (19 May)
Redesigned engine, but power unchanged at 30bhp: crankcase with detachable dynamo pedestal; compression ratio raised from 6.1:1 to 6.6:1; modified cylinder heads, camshaft and pushrods; crankshaft pulley/fan ratio changed from 1:2 to 1:1.75. One-piece 'tunnel' transmission introduced.
483 965 (Jun)
Dynamo uprated from 160 watt to 180 watt.
484 000 approx (30 Jun)
Hole for starting handle deleted from rear valance.

1960
570 016 (Feb)
Front wheel bearings lubricated with lithium grease A-1060 instead of universal grease A-052.
575 830 (Feb)
Resistor type plug leads replace suppressed sparking plug connectors.
579 519 (Mar)
Stronger windscreen wiper motor with increased blade pressure.
614 456 (1 Jun)
Engine rated at 34bhp: Solex 28PCI carburettor replaced by 28PICT, and compression ratio increased from 6.6:1 to 7.0:1. Oil bath air cleaner now with pre-heating. Speedometer re-calibrated to 120kph. Non-US models now with flashing indicators instead of semaphores.
624 263 (Jun)
Thickness of dynamo pulley increased from 2mm to 2.5mm.
639 531 (Aug)
Two marks on crankshaft pulley for ignition timing (7.5 degrees and 10 degrees BTDC); previously one mark at 7.5 degrees.
678 336 (Nov)
Throttle cable eye hooked directly into hole in pedal arm. Previously secured with bolt, washer and cotter pin.
679 977 (Nov)
Number of blades on cooling fan increased from 16 to 28.
705 620 (29 Dec)
Top hinges on side doors placed slightly lower.

1961
716 433 (Jan)
Gasket placed between fuel filter and pump cover, and filter modified.
770 290 (May)
Bi-metal exhaust valves for North American market.
784 631 (Jun)
Grab handles on central row of seats in Kombi and Microbuses changed from tubular steel to ridged plastic.
792 098 (Jun)
Connection hose from oil filler to air cleaner in place of breather tube, for improved crankcase ventilation.
793 372 (Jun)
Pushrod seals of white plastic instead of red and green rubber.
794 677 (Jun)
Bi-metal exhaust valves standardised.
803 000 (Jul)
Upper corners of speedometer binnacle become more rounded, grab handle for passenger side of dashboard.
803 456 (Jul)
Indicator warning lights in speedometer changed from red to green.
815 634 (Aug)
Flat front indicators for US vehicles; larger tail lamp units with separate indicator lens in amber (Europe) or (red) US; two padded sun visors for all models; headlamp dipswitch

COLOUR SCHEMES

MICROBUS AND SAMBA

UPPER BODY	LOWER BODY	MICROBUS UPHOLSTERY	SAMBA UPHOLSTERY
MAR 1950 TO FEB 1955 **(chassis 20 00 001 to 20 117 901)**			
Brown Beige (L76)	Light Beige (L75)	Beige	–
Stone Grey (L221)	Stone Grey (L221)	Beige	–
Chestnut Brown (L73)	Sealing Wax Red (L53)	–	Black
MAR 1955 TO JUL 1958 **(chassis 20 117 902 to 374 810)**			
Palm Green (L312)	Sand Green (L311)	Soft green (77)	–
Sand Green (L260)	Sand Grey (L260)	Light Brown (76)	–
Chestnut Brown (L73)	Sealing Wax Red (L53)	–	Light Brown (76)
AUG 1958 TO FEB 1961 **(chassis 374 811 to 749 000)**			
Seagull Grey (L347)	Mango Green (L346)	Caramel Brown (76)	–
Pearl Grey (L21)	Pearl Grey (L21)	Caramel Brown (76)	Blue-Grey (77)
Beige Grey (L472)	Sealing Wax Red (L53)	–	Blue-Grey (77)
MAR 1961 TO JUL 1964 **(chassis 749 001 to 1 328 871)**			
Blue White (L289/17)	Turquoise (L380/42)	Como Green (81)	Como Green (81)
Pearl White (L87/13)	Mouse Grey (L325/43)	Basalt Grey (80)	Basalt Grey (80)
Beige Grey (L472/44)	Sealing Wax Red (L53/45)	Basalt Grey (80)	Silver Beige (75)
AUG 1964 TO JUL 1965 **(chassis 215 000 001 to 215 190 000)**			
Blue White (L289/17)	Sea Blue (L360/12)	Mesh Grey (83)	Mesh Grey (83)
Blue White (L289/17)	Velvet Green (L512/38)	Mesh Grey (83)	Mesh Grey (83)
Beige Grey (L472/44)	Sealing Wax Red (L53/45)	Mesh Grey (83)	Mesh Grey (83)
AUG 1965 TO JUL 1967 **(chassis 216 000 001 to 217 148 459)**			
Cumulus White (L680/18)	Sea Blue (L360/12)	Mesh Grey (83)	Aero Papyrus White (72)
Pearl White (L87/13)	Velvet Green (L512/38)	Mesh Grey (83)	Mesh Platinum (70)
Beige Grey (L472/44)	Titian Red (L555/43)	Mesh Grey (83)	Mesh Platinum (70)
Lotus White (L282/42)	Lotus White (L282/42)	Mesh Grey (83)	Aero Balearic (71)

KOMBI AND COMMERCIALS

BODY	UPHOLSTERY	BODY	UPHOLSTERY
MAR 1950 TO FEB 1953 **(chassis 20 00 001 to 20 46 563)**		**MAR 1953 TO JUL 1958** **(chassis 20 46 564 to 374 810)**	
Pearl Grey (L21)	Black	Pearl Grey (L21)	Black
Medium Grey (L22)	Black	Grey (L28)	Black
Dove Blue (L31)	Black	Dove Blue (L31)	Black
Chestnut Brown (L73)	Black	Ivory (L52)	Black
Brown-Beige (L76)	Black		
		SEP 1961 TO JUL 1963 **(chassis 835 180 to 1 144 281)**	
AUG 1958 TO AUG 1961 **(chassis 374 811 to 835 179)**			
		Dove Blue (L31)	Grey (80)
		Ivory (L52)	Grey (80)
Dove Blue (L31)	Grey (80)	Pearl White (L87)	Grey (80)
Sealing Wax Red (L53)	Grey (80)	Light Grey (L345)	Grey (80)
Ivory (L52)	Grey (80)	Turquoise (L380)	Grey (80)
Light Grey (L345)	Grey (80)	Ruby Red (L456)	Grey (80)
AUG 1963 TO JUL 1964 **(chassis 1 144 282 to 1 328 271)**		**AUG 1964 TO JUL 1967** **(chassis 215 000 001 to 217 148 459)**	
Dove Blue (L31/40)	Grey (80)		
Ivory (L52/46)	Grey (80)	Dove Blue (L31/40)	Mesh Grey (83)
Pearl White (L87/13)	Grey (80)	Ivory (L567/46)	Mesh Grey (83)
Light Grey (L345/41)	Grey (80)	Pearl White (L87/13)	Mesh Grey (83)
Turquoise (L380/42)	Grey (80)	Light Grey (L345/41)	Mesh Grey (83)
Ruby Red (L456/11)	Grey (80)	Velvet Green (L512/38)	Mesh Grey (83)

PRODUCTION FIGURES

Year	Panelvan	Microbus	Samba	Kombi	Pick-up	Ambulance	Others	Total
1949	6	1		1				(8)[1]
1950	5662	1142	-	1254	1	-	-	8059
1951	6049	2805	269	2843	1	36	-	12003
1952	9353	4052	1142	5031	1606	481	-	21665
1953	11190	4086	1289	5753	5741	358	-	28417
1954	14550	5693	1937	8868	8562	589	-	40119
1955	17577	7957	2195	11346	10138	694	-	49907
1956	22657	9726	2072	16010	11449	586	-	62500
1957	30683	17197	3514	23495	16450	644	-	91983
1958	36672	19499	4342	21732	19142	486	-	101873[2]
1959	41395	22943	6241	25699	24465	710	-	121453[2]
1960	47498	22504	7846	30425	30988	658	-	139919[2]
1961	45121	25410	8095	35950	36822	883	4	152285[2]
1962	47237	29898	11280	38506	38118	728	7	165774
1963	47891	31196	14764	40882	39458	675	-	174866
1964	48481	40115	14031	44659	39832	829	-	187947
1965	43723	37933	12467	44331	37444	864	-	176762
1966	43084	30767	18790	46284	36534	816	-	176275
1967	Figures cannot be broken down							c68100[3]
Total								c1833000[4]

[1] 'Type 29' prototypes
[2] c52900 CKD kits additionally built in 1958-61 period
[3] 1967 production is an estimate, model split not possible
[4] Total is for German production at Wolfsburg and Hanover; additionally vehicles were built in Brazil (until 1975, c400,000), South Africa and Australia (until 1968, c35,000).

moved forward 100mm (3.9in) on right-hand drive versions, front board and mat modified correspondingly.

829 682 (Sep)
Maintenance-free tie rods on left-hand drive vehicles. Formerly with grease nipples.

1962
889 352 (Jan)
Distributor vacuum unit fitted with vacuum pipe with loop between distributor and carburettor in place of tube.

891 205 (Jan)
Speedometer cable enclosed in metal casing with plastic sheathing instead of plastic tube as previously.

896 577 (Feb)
Paper gasket seated between reduction gear housing cover and brake back plate.

915 559 (Mar)
Outer surface of inlet manifold and pre-heater pipe treated with zinc paint instead of being phosphated as previously.

928 307 (Apr)
Fuel pipe between pump and carburettor fitted with hose connecting pieces.

934 616 (Apr)
Oil filler drain passage, diameter up from 3mm to 6mm.

971 550 (Aug)
Front bench seat replaced by separate but close-coupled seats for driver and passenger(s); gearbox casing modified to accept 200mm clutch.

1 021 547 (Nov)
Windscreen wiper motor mounted at two points instead of three as previously.

1963
1 041 014 (7 Jan)
First 1500 engine, initially only available for US.

1 080 104 (Mar)
Ten engine cooling louvres instead of nine, modified to face inwards instead of outwards.

1 140 022 (Jul)
US speedometers marked with gearchange points.

1 144 303 (Aug)
Wider rear window in wider tailgate (causing rear quarter windows to be dropped from Microbus de luxe, creating '21-window' version); flat front indicators for European vehicles; tailgate locking changed from T handle to push-button, with appropriate finger room indented in panel below. Driven gear shaft in reduction gearbox increased in diameter from 30mm to 35mm. First gear wheel increased in width from 11.80mm to 13.55mm.

1 146 027 (Aug)
Air correction jet modified from 145 y to 150 z on 28 PICT carburettor (1500 model).

1 197 411 (Nov)
Oil bath air cleaner mounted on right in upper engine compartment instead of left as previously.

1 197 853 (Nov)

Suspension spring plate fixing bolts secured with spring washers instead of lock plates.

1 222 026 (Dec)
New cab door handles with push-button operation.

1964
1 238 208 (1200), 1 238 882 (1500) (Jan)
Diameter of number one bearing journal reduced by 0.005mm.

1 259 098 (Mar)
Solex 28 PICT carburettor fitted with larger automatic choke.

1 296 714 (May)
Bosch RSIVA 200/6/3 regulator modified for reduced voltage drop.

000 001 (3 Aug)
Larger windscreen wiper blades fitted; windscreen washers with pneumatic operation for plastic reservoir.

019 890 (Sep)
Heat exchangers on 1200 ribbed internally and warm air hose increased in diameter from 55mm to 60mm.

035 391 (Sep)
White vinyl headlining standard on Types 22 and 24.

068 247 (Dec)
Champion L 87 y sparking plugs fitted, but Bosch W 175 T1, Beru 175/14 and Champion L85 still used.

1965
112 887 (Feb)
Drilling for oil pocket in crankshaft bearing shell number two increased in diameter from 4mm to 5mm.

000 001 (Aug)
Oil filler neck enlarged, windscreen wiper motor with two speeds, headlamp dipswitch transferred from floor to steering column, engine lid opened by push-button with finger grip; new interior cab door handles. Wider rear cab window and revised pattern of inward-facing engine cooling louvres on Pick-ups.

1966
083 208 (Jan)
Heater tube in left-hand heat exchanger made seamless instead of welded in two pieces.

113 501 (Mar)
Flanges for attaching oil cooler reinforced.

000 001 (Aug)
12-volt electrics introduced. Flywheel enlarged with 130 teeth instead of 109, gearbox case modified for larger 12-volt starter motor. Tailgate opened by new push-button with finger grip, panel indent below deleted.

045 893 (Oct)
Hose between carburettor and fuel pump secured with clips.

067 544 (Dec)
Crankcase halves sealing compound changed from dark grey to light brown.

BAY-WINDOW (1967-79)
CHASSIS NUMBER DATING

1968 model year		1969 model year	
Aug 1	218 000 001	Aug 1	219 000 001
Dec 31	218 073 585	Dec 31	219 098 974
Jul 31	218 202 251	Jul 31	219 238 131

1970 model year		1971 model year	
1 Aug	210 000 0001	Aug 1	211 2 000 001
Dec 31	210 2 106 747	Dec 31	211 2 114 988
Jul 31	210 2 248 837	Jul 31	211 2 276 560

1972 model year		1973 model year	
Aug 1	212 2 000 001	Aug 1	213 2 000 001
Dec 31	212 2 088 996	Dec 31	213 2 102 496
Jul 31	212 2 246 946	Jul 31	213 2 254 657

1974 model year		1975 model year	
Aug 1	214 2 000 001	Aug 1	215 2 000 001
Dec 31	214 2 094 429	Dec 31	215 2 073 083
Jul 31	214 2 194 943	Jul 31	215 2 155 145

1976 model year		1977 model year	
Aug 1	216 2 000 001	Aug 1	217 2 000 001
Dec 31	216 2 077 675	Dec 31	217 2 081 316
Jul 31	216 2 ??? ???	Jul 31	217 2 ??? ???

1978 model year		1979 model year	
Aug 1	218 2 000 001	Aug 1	219 2 000 001
Dec 31	218 2 072 273	Dec 31	219 2 073 637
Jul 31	218 2 ??? ???	Jul 31	219 2 153 964

Note First two digits represent model type: numbers found are 21 (Panelvan), 22 (Microbus eight-seater), 23 (Kombi), 24 (Clipper or Microbus L eight-seater), 25 (Microbus L seven-seater), 26 (Pick-up), 27 (Ambulance) and 28 (Microbus seven-seater). The third digit represents the model year. From 1970, the fourth digit is always a '2', representing the '2nd generation of Transporters' or simply 'T2'.

PRODUCTION CHANGES

1968 model year
000 001 (Aug 67)
Beginning of Bay-window production. Brand new model with much larger body than previously, panoramic one-piece windscreen, sliding side door as standard, dual-circuit brakes, double-jointed rear swing axles for safer roadholding and now without reduction gearboxes in rear hubs. Revised dashboard, switchgear in softer, flatter plastic, more comprehensive instrumentation, more powerful single-port 1600 engine.

1969 model year
000 001 (Aug 68)
Cab door handle design changed, now with trigger release.

1970 model year
2 000 001 (Aug 69)
Side-mounted direction indicators and reversing lights for some export markets, side reflectors change from circular to square on US models, ignition starter without steering lock optional on Microbuses, oil strainer plate without central nut, oil pump relief valves and springs strengthened, stronger oil cooler sealing washer, torsion bars and anti-roll bar strengthened, four bolt holes on each side of front torsion beam for attaching to chassis spaced further apart (previous beams not interchangeable).

1971 model year
2 000 001 (Aug 70)
Front disc brakes introduced, five-stud fixings and wheel design changed to suit; brake pressure regulator fitted to rear brakes to help equalise front/rear pressure under heavy braking. 1600 engine modified with twin-port cylinder heads, exhaust system modified to further aid engine 'breathing'; oil cooler alloy instead of steel to help heat dissipation, fan housing modified correspondingly.

2 138 001
Oil pump uprated and oil pump shaft modified.

2 300 000 (Jul 71)
Eberspächer stationary petrol heater discontinued on Ambulance and fire tender. Reversing lamps available for High-roof Panelvan and Double-cab Pick-up.

1972 model year
2 000 001 (Aug 1971)
Larger 1700 engine optionally available for all models except Pick-up (but standard for all models in US), engine cooling louvres enlarged to suit. Longer oil dipstick, front engine tinware cover plate reshaped for improved engine cooling, multi-pin socket in engine compartment for electronic fault diagnosis, exhaust system with filter extension, rear torsion bars marked with green paint, rear wheel brake cylinder diameter increased to 23.81mm. Larger tail-lamps, fuel filler flap moved further back to avoid overlap with sliding side door. Opening quarterlights available for rear side windows in Double-cab Pick-up.
2 088 996
Headlamp flasher with simultaneous function for number plate light, and lockable fuel filler cap (Austria).
2 161 958
Strainer fitted inside brake fluid reservoir.
2 300 000 (Jul 72)
Retaining clip on heater connector hose discontinued. Steering box casing changed from cast iron to cast alloy, higher cab seat backrests.

1973 model year
2 000 001 (Aug 72)
Front indicators moved from below to above headlamps, VW nose roundel reduced in size and placed lower on front panel, revised bumpers without cab step at front, fuel filler flap deleted (leaving filler cap exposed), shallower engine lid with revised number plate light housing, sliding door handle modified and panel recess behind changed to suit. Recessed piston crowns for 1600 engine, three-speed automatic gearbox introduced with 1700 engine only. Worm and roller steering replaces worm and peg. Calibrated differential for fitment of tachograph on commercial vehicles. Seat backrests with mountings for head restraints, detachable front head restraints fitted to Microbuses as extra-cost option, trim fitted around heater vents, brake fluid reservoir moved from under dashboard to below base of driver's seat, brake discs made wider and stub axles lengthened. Cab floor redesigned to incorporate 'crumple' zone.
2 300 000 (Jul 73)
Eberspächer stationary petrol heater discontinued on High-roof Panelvan and Kombi (not all markets).

1974 model year
2 000 001 (Aug 73)
Larger 1800 engine supersedes 1700, with Bosch Jetronic fuel injection for US market; flywheel on 1800 with automatic transmission changed for drive plate. Compliance with exhaust emission standards on vehicles for Sweden and Japan; convex exterior door mirror for Japan; laminated windscreen for Sweden. Automatic three-point seat belt for driver's seat and lap belt for passenger's (LHD). Secondary air control valve on twin carburettor engines modified (Australia). Fuel filler neck modified on Panelvan, Ambulance and Kombi. Headlamp washers introduced as extra-cost option, halogen headlamp bulbs fitted as standard. Heated rear window optional on Microbus, sliding side door striker plate modified, tinted glass for Kombis and Microbuses at extra cost.
2 110 465
Gear lever base and bush simplified.
2 164 060
Sheer bolt incorporated into steering column.
2 300 000 (Jul 74)
Air cleaner with additional cyclone filter discontinued on Pick-ups.
2 300 009 (Jul 74)
Air filter system with two air cleaners for some export markets.

1975 model year
2 000 001 (Aug 74)
Exhaust emission control equipment introduced on High-roof Panelvan and Kombi. Clock with pre-selector timer on LHD vehicles, special cloth upholstery available at extra cost in vehicles exported to Denmark. Alternator fitted to

Panelvan, Kombi and Ambulance. Halogen foglamps and intermittent wash/wipe facility for home market only. Seal for deflector plate in engine cooling tinware modified. Electrical system fully suppressed. Different waistline bright trim on Luxury Microbus: position lowered, rubber insert added, continuation across tail deleted.
2 300 000 (Jul 75)
Modified carburettor seating gasket, yellow headlamp bulbs for French market discontinued. Cloth upholstery available in Microbuses instead of vinyl, but not in all markets.

1976 model year
2 000 001 (Aug 75)
2-litre engine becomes available. Differential housing and crownwheel and pinion modified. Full-width partition between cab and load area in High-roof Panelvan and Microbus for Austrian market. Fan housing and rubber grommets in engine cooling tinware modified in shape. Base of accelerator pedal modified in shape. Fuel pump gaskets improved. Lock ring, washer, hexagonal nut and sealing washers in exhaust system modified. Smaller hinges for engine lid; tailgate and engine lid locks in black plastic instead of chromed metal.
2 077 583
Air cleaner thermostat to control intake air pre-heating replaced by temperature sensor to vary volume of fuel according to ambient temperature.
2 077 584
Deceleration and throttle valve switch in fuel injection system improved.
2 078 000
Swivelling driver's seat available as extra-cost option in Panelvan, Microbus and Kombi.

Original handbook and close-up of perforated white vinyl upholstery from a Microbus.

2 119 000
K-Jetronic fuel injection fitted to RHD versions.

1977 model year
2 000 001 (Aug 76)
Compliance with exhaust emissions standards (Australia).

1978 model year
2 000 001 (Aug 77)
Steering wheel with thicker rim and spokes. Sliding side window in sliding door and opposite side available for Ambulance, Kombi and Microbus. Heated rear window available for Kombi.

COLOUR SCHEMES

Body colours by model year

Neptune Blue	1968-72
Pearl White	1968
Lotus White	1968-70
Light Grey	1968-72
Velvet Green	1968-70
Titian Red	1968
Ivory	1968-72
Savanna Beige	1968-70
Montana Red	1969-70
Brilliant Blue	1969-70
Delta Green	1969-70
Sierra Yellow	1971-72
Chianti Red	1971-72
Niagara Blue	1971-72
Elm Green	1971-72
Pastel White	1971-72
Kansas Beige	1971-72
Ceylon Beige	1973-78
Brilliant Orange	1973-79
Kansas Red	1973-75
Neptune Blue	1973-79
Orient Blue	1973-75
Sumatra Green	1973-78
Light Grey	1973-79
Ivory	1973-79
Bali Yellow	1974-75
Marino Yellow	1974-79
Taiga Green	1974-79
Senegal Red	1976-79
Oceanic Blue	1976-79
Atlas White	1977
Agata Brown	1977-79
Panama Brown	1978-79
Dakota Beige	1978
Date Brown	1978
Fox Red	1978
Diamond Silver Metallic	1976-79
Mexico Beige	1979

Contrast roof colours by model year

Cloud White	1968-70
Pastel White	1971-78
Black	1971-72

PRODUCTION FIGURES

Year	Panelvan	Microbus	Kombi	Pick-up	Double-cab	Ambulance	Others	Total
1967	Figures cannot be broken down							c73500[1]
1968	50880	64411	68597	31070	12091	1241	-	228290
1969	54929	64326	77956	31296	15152	1270	16	244945
1970	53759	71719	87391	28340	15393	1242	29	257873
1971	47913	74850	87136	24639	14896	1357	11	250802
1972	56119	66400	90712	27175	16829	1860	6	259101
1973	56866	58442	87849	25490	15506	2023	1	246177
1974	39822	38700	64027	17715	12082	1762	13	174121
1975	39392	29062	63928	14808	11043	1699	-	159752
1976	45263	31390	65799	14014	11807	1221	-	169494
1977	40008	38068	55245	14139	12115	1411	-	160986
1978	40454	34331	52251	12694	13396	1310	-	154436
1979	28569	13566	31732	5667	5475	623	-	85632
Total								c2465000[2]

[1] 1967 production is an estimate
[2] Total is for German production at Hanover and Emden; additionally vehicles were built in Brazil, South Africa, Australia and Mexico (dates and figures unknown).